"UNTO THIS LAST"

"Unto This Last"

Four Essays

on the First Principles of Political Economy

JOHN RUSKIN

Edited with an introduction by Lloyd J. Hubenka

UNIVERSITY OF NEBRASKA PRESS · LINCOLN

Publishers on the Plains

UNP

Manufactured in the United States of America

Contents

Editor's Introduction

IN THE autumn of 1860, four short essays on political economy bearing the strange title *"Unto This Last"* appeared in *Cornhill Magazine*. Their author identified himself only by his initials, J. R.; but the style of the essays and their object made even the initials superfluous, for readers immediately recognized the work of John Ruskin. That the educated English public had no difficulty identifying the author is perhaps testimony to what Ruskin had achieved in almost twenty years of hard work. With the publication of the first volume of *Modern Painters* in 1843, he had begun a struggle to revivify English art criticism as well as to purge English art of the conventionalism which marked the paintings of Eastlake, Maclise, Dyce, and Mulready and of the sentimentalism and superficiality of the German school of art made popular in England by Queen Victoria's consort, Prince Albert of Saxe-Coburg-Gotha. Although Ruskin waged his campaign single-handed and against enormous odds, he did not waver from his purpose. The second volume of *Modern Painters*, appearing in 1846, was followed by *The Seven Lamps of Architecture* (1849), *The Stones of Venice* (1851, 1853), and the three remaining volumes of *Modern Painters* (1856, 1860). While this exertion left him shattered in mind and body, by 1860 he had largely persuaded English intellectuals to accept his views about art. Indeed, one critic lauded him as a "Luther of the arts" and

vii

another referred to him as "speaking, as if ever a man spoke, by the spirit and approval of heaven."[1]

These same intellectuals, however, were not so certain that the essays in *Cornhill Magazine* bore the stamp of heavenly approval. Instead of being treatises on art or architecture, the essays were polemics against the principles of the prevailing political economy of the day. To some extent, the educated English public had been prepared for this assault by Ruskin's *Political Economy of Art* (1857); but while his digressions on current commercial operations showed considerable hostility towards utilitarian economics,[2] the work was still overlaid with a veneer of art. Now, however, the veneer was off and cries of anguish and horror were heard everywhere. After reading the first of the essays, Dante Gabriel Rossetti, whom Ruskin had befriended, asked an acquaintance, "Who *could* read it, or anything about such bosh!"[3] Moreover, the press which had lavished praise on his art criticism now cut him to pieces. A critic for *The Saturday Review*, August 4, 1860, for example, dismissed the leading propositions of the first essay as "total absurdity"; writing of all four essays on November 10, 1860, he asserted they were "absolute nonsense . . . dashed with a sort of milk and water asceticism" and that Adam Smith, Ricardo, and Mill were entitled "to better treatment than . . . to be preached to death by a mad governess." Another reviewer, in the November 1860 issue of *Frazer's Magazine*, titled his piece "Political Economy in the Clouds," explaining that "the Clouds are Mr. Ruskin's Muses. The vapoury goddesses reveal themselves in everything he writes."

This outcry in the press coupled with the numerous letters of

1. As quoted in *The Works of John Ruskin*, eds. E. T. Cook and A. Wedderburn (London: George Allen, 1904), V, lx. All subsequent references to Ruskin's works will be to this Library Edition unless otherwise noted. The laudatory comments about Ruskin's art criticism appeared in the *Oxford and Cambridge Magazine* in April and June, 1856.

2. Throughout this introduction, I use "utilitarian economics" and "classical economics" as synonymous terms.

3. Oswald Doughty, *Dante Gabriel Rossetti* (New Haven: Yale University Press, 1949), p. 284.

protest from subscribers did not go unnoticed by William Make-peace Thackeray, the editor of *Cornhill Magazine*. When the storm became too much for him to endure, he wrote apologetically to Ruskin that he could admit only one essay more, and with Thackeray's permission the last essay, "*Ad Valorem*," was made a little longer than the rest. Ruskin was deeply hurt by this public reprobation. He had planned to write an extended series of essays on political economy which he hoped might perhaps be taken up by some political group, much as Disraeli's political ideas had been taken up by the Young England Movement. But now he realized that at least among the educated middle class he no longer had an audience. As Carlyle told him, they had become a minority of two against the "dismal science." For a time Ruskin thought of leaving England for good and settling somewhere on the Continent. But as the months passed he became increasingly convinced of the truth of his social message and resolved that the central work of his life would be to write an exhaustive treatise on political economy. "What message I have given," he wrote to Charles Eliot Norton in 1861, "is all wrong: has to be all re-said, in another way, and is, so said, almost too terrible to be serviceable."[4]

In 1862, he collected the *Cornhill Magazine* essays, added a preface, and reissued them without alteration. But "*Unto This Last*" fared no better in book form than it had in the magazine. Indeed, it was so poorly received that ten years later Smith Elder & Co., Ruskin's publishers, still had copies for sale from the original printing. In that same year, 1862, still hopeful of persuading the British public to accept his views on political economy, Ruskin published a second series of essays, this time in *Frazer's Magazine*, to which he later gave the title *Munera Pulveris*. They met with the same fate as the earlier essays. Although sales of his earlier works on art declined sharply because of the essays on political economy, he continued to address himself to

4. *Letters of John Ruskin to Charles Eliot Norton* (Boston: Houghton Mifflin, 1905), I, 118–119.

socioeconomic questions. In 1865, he published *Sesame and Lilies*; in 1866, *The Ethics of the Dust* and *The Crown of Wild Olive*; in 1867, *Time and Tide*; and from 1871 through 1884, *Fors Clavigera*—all dealing either wholly or in part with what he conceived to be the needed reforms of industrial society. Convinced that his social treatises were the only works in his canon worthy of public attention, Ruskin allowed several of his earlier books on art to go out of print and began to reprint extracts from *"Unto This Last"* and other of his socioeconomic studies in inexpensive editions in order to make them available to the British workman. In 1871, attempting to put his social ideas into practice, he founded the Guild of St. George to show what should be done to educate the laborer and "to divert a little of the large current of English charity and justice from watching disease to guarding health, and from the punishment of crime to the reward of virtue; to establish, here and there, exercise grounds instead of hospitals, and training schools instead of penitentiaries."[5] Although he gave his time and a tenth of his fortune to this project, the Guild was as much a failure as his books on economics. It was not until 1885, twenty-five years after the publication of *"Unto This Last,"* that his services to economics were publicly recognized by the presentation of an Address signed by several of the foremost economists of the day. But this accolade came too late; in 1878 Ruskin had suffered the first attack of the madness which was to destroy him.

More than a hundred years have passed since the essays were first published and one may rightly ask what significance they have for the modern reader. Our economic philosophy is no longer informed by the doctrines of classical economists such as John Stuart Mill or David Ricardo, and the socioeconomic problems of the 1850's and 1860's—the inhuman housing, the appalling working conditions, the unjust wage scales—have long since been ameliorated. Indeed, to the modern reader the specific political

5. *Works*, XXVII, p. 158.

reforms advocated by Ruskin in the Preface to *"Unto This Last"* no doubt seem to be the most obvious commonplaces of the welfare state. We have vocational schools, Medicare, the Job Corps, Social Security, and a host of other welfare programs which the stimulus of Ruskin's social philosophy helped to bring into existence. But the significance of *"Unto This Last"* for our time—and for ages to come—does not lie in Ruskin's attack on a nineteenth-century school of economic thought or in the specific welfare measures he proposes; its value resides in Ruskin's critique of our conception of wealth and of the ethical foundations of our industrial civilization. He invites us to look closely at our affluence: to ask ourselves among other things how wealth is achieved in our economic paradise, how it is spent, and what effect it has on the lives of the citizenry of a nation. Uncommon questions these, but certainly they are not irrelevant.

Obviously these are the questions of a moralist, not a political ideologue; and in an age accustomed to political panaceas, Ruskin's social philosophy with its stress on the need for a right condition of the human heart must seem sentimental. In reality his social thought is more radical than that which we have received from the liberals. The liberal—both in this century and the last— generally has been satisfied with the premises and assumptions upon which capitalist society is founded. His aim has been to correct the disorders of the capitalist system: to insure through social legislation that in our competitive society every man has an equal opportunity to be a winner and the right to determine for himself what constitutes the prize. Ruskin's quarrel, however, is not with the disorders of capitalism but with the order itself. He passionately believes that the capitalistic civilization is immoral, vicious, and brutalizing. He wishes to demolish it but, unlike Marx or Bakunin, he does not call for revolution. In many respects Ruskin's conflict with his age is so profound that it transcends any political remedies. His social philosophy resembles Tolstoy's in that he is convinced that the reformation of the social order can not be brought about from without. Parliaments, legislatures, political parties, pressure groups, political societies, trade unions—all the instruments through which the discontented normally try to affect social change—Ruskin distrusts and considers unessential. He shares Toltoy's conviction that it is possible to remove the evils of the world only by individual change of heart; and his cry is "Go and reform yourself before you try to reform the social order." To the politically sophisticated, Ruskin, in taking this stand, offers them a providential opportunity to display their own brilliance. To be sure, Ruskin seems unaware that certain social situations make it impossible for a man to reform himself or, worse, make such a reformation irrelevant. Yet, as Leslie Stephens has said, reading Ruskin we have the uncomfortable feeling that he may be more essentially in the right than we would care to admit. If the political experience of the 1960's has taught us any lesson at all, it is that social legislation does very little in itself to produce social peace, let alone social harmony. Perhaps our error has been to focus our attention on passing laws which will guarantee rights and not on the hearts of the men who must make the social organism work. In Ruskin's view, a society of righteous men makes social reform easy if not unnecessary; and to suggest how we may achieve a right condition of the heart, he puts before us the most radical precepts ever given man: "Love thy neighbor as thyself"; "Do unto others as you would have others do unto you." How much more radical these precepts are than any pronouncements made by liberal pundits would be apparent to anyone who attempted to live by them in our acquisitive society.

II

Ruskin was not the first man in his age to cry out against the industrial system nor was he the first to call for a moral rather than a political reformation of nineteenth-century English society. His social philosophy, while highly original in some ways, is part of a distinct tradition of social criticism which makes its way down through the century. This tradition, for lack of a better term, may be called "transcendental" in that those who shared this tendency of mind believed that there existed sanctions of a higher order than Benthamite individualism. While the transcendentalists were no less desirous of reforming society than were utilitarians such as Jeremy Bentham or David Ricardo, they disagreed with them over what was to be reformed and how reform was to be achieved. They did not, for example, believe in the ideal of democracy nor were they convinced of the efficacy of reform by abstract formulas. Being in the main Romantic poets and essayists rather than social scientists, they put their faith in truth derived from the intuitive and spiritual elements of the human mind and felt that this truth gave those who trusted it a special insight into the ultimate questions of existence. And if the wisdom gained from such an insight told them anything, it demonstrated that the civilization of nineteenth-century England was corrupt. In their view neither legislation nor political reform would materially improve society; indeed, they believed that the measures proposed by the liberals in Parliament to further the aims and hopes of democratic and capitalist society, would probably make society a good deal worse. To the transcendentalists, it was precisely this sort of society, with its emphasis on individual liberties and the pursuit of money, which had corrupted the social order. They saw no way out of the dilemma except to reform the human heart. Until that reform took place, until men were once again willing to live as brothers and put communal interests above their own, they held out little hope for the amelioration of the human condition.

Thus in opposition to the atomistic, competitive, and mechanistic civilization which was rapidly rising up about them, the transcendentalists tried to revivify the communal devotion to the ideals of cooperation and human solidarity which had irradiated the pre-industrial and pre-capitalist civilization of the Middle Ages. It was in an attempt to answer the political ideology of James Mill that Samuel Taylor Coleridge, the intellectual parent of these critics, declared in his *On the Constitution of Church and State* (1830) that society was an organism, a commonwealth in which the continuing health of the whole was more important than the welfare of the individual or any class. Robert Owen, another reformer in this tradition of social reform, established at his mill at New Lanark a "Plan" in which his workers, instead of being the instruments of his own gain, were gathered into "Villages of Cooperation," very similar to the Undershaft Cooperative in Shaw's *Major Barbara*, where education was provided for the children of the workers and where the workers themselves shared in the profits. After Coleridge and Owen, the transcendental line of attack was carried on by two disciples of Coleridge—Thomas Carlyle and Frederick Denison Maurice. Carlyle's *Sartor Resartus* (1831) attests to his passionate conviction that all men are brothers, united to each other by "organic filaments," and *Past and Present* (1843) is an indictment of the Mammon of Unrighteousness which he found dominating the Victorian ethos. Maurice waged his war against the utilitarians and the classical economists upon a more religious plane. He envisioned a spiritual society in which all men and all sects were united in a society which he referred to as "the full and all embracing ocean of the Catholic Church," and it was in an effort to bring such a church into being that he began the Christian Socialist movement in 1848.

By 1860, however, these early transcendentalists had reached the end of their tether. Coleridge and Owen were dead. Carlyle, now sixty-five, was to make only one more assault on the Victorian social order with his essay *Shooting Niagara—and After* (1867). Because of the workers' unresponsiveness and the public's absorption in the Crimean War, Maurice's Christian Socialist movement failed, and Maurice himself soon became embroiled in theological controversies which were to monopolize his energies. It was thus Ruskin who carried on the transcendental attack against the "dismal science" in the last forty years of the century. Under his leadership the transcendentalist line of attack underwent a significant change: Ruskin led his followers to social reform through art. Until the appearance of *The Stones of Venice* (1851, 1853) there was very little interest in art and aesthetics among those of the transcendental attitude of mind. Maurice, for example, was primarily a theologian; and when he turned to social reform, he did so with the idea of bringing into being a society that conformed with his interpretation of the meaning of Christianity. And while Carlyle, like Ruskin, admired the Middle Ages, his praise for the period was restricted largely to its political structure. Hence those phenomena of the late nineteenth century —the Guild of St. Matthew and the Church and Stage Guild, which aimed to further both human solidarity and art—owe their inspiration to Ruskin more than anyone. Through his writings and through the example of his own Guild of St. George, he showed a generation of intellectuals that social reform involved more than economics. Besides giving the British Labor Party its distinctly moral and humanitarian character, Ruskin made it clear to sensitive and artistic young men such as William Morris, Bernard Shaw, and Stewart Headlam[6] that social reform was not only an ethical and religious but also an artistic necessity, that not only was the heart of nineteenth-century England desperately wicked but also that great art would not be possible again until conditions were set aright.

Although no two spheres of human activity would appear to be farther apart than art criticism and political economy, in Ruskin's case the first is the causal antecedent of the second, for it was by a natural course of development rather than by any sudden change of idea that the art critic of *Modern Painters* I became the social prophet of *"Unto This Last."* In *The Romantic Quest*, Hoxie Neale Fairchild distinguishes between two elements in the Romantic temperament. One is transcendentalism; the other he calls descendentalism and defines as the love on the part of the Romantics "to burrow deeply into the actual."[7] In Ruskin, as in Carlyle, both elements manifest themselves. But whereas in Carlyle's work they are interfused from the beginning, in Ruskin's the latter, his love and interest in the beauty of this world, appears more markedly at first. It is only as he becomes

6. Stewart Headlam (1847–1924) was a Christian Socialist, a member of the Fabian Society, and the founder of the Guild of St. Matthew (1877) and the Church and Stage Guild (1879).

7. Hoxie Neale Fairchild, *The Romantic Quest* (Philadelphia: Albert Saider, 1931), p. 141.

increasingly disturbed by what he sees in the actual world and less certain of its religious meaning that the transcendental side of his nature comes to the fore.

The nature of his upbringing largely determined that he would first respond to the actual and reveal most emphatically in his early works the descendental side of his temperament. The only child of a well-to-do London wine merchant, Ruskin grew up in virtual isolation. He lived in a closely-guarded, conventional, and narrowly religious home where toys and amusements were forbidden and the few visitors were either relatives or business friends of his father. His childhood days, as he explains in his autobiographical work *Praeterita* (1885), were spent "contentedly in tracing the squares and comparing the colours of my carpet" or in "counting the bricks in the opposite houses."[8] His parents, devout Evangelicals, devoted their time and energies to training their son for academic distinction and later, his mother hoped, a career in the Church. The only breaks in this almost monastic life were yearly trips through rural England and, later on, journeys to the more scenic areas of Europe. The first of these European trips was prompted by an event which was to determine the main tenor of his life. On his thirteenth birthday, in 1833, he was given a copy of Rogers's *Italy* with vignettes by the great English landscape painter J. M. W. Turner. Ruskin, who had acquired an appreciation for solitary natural scenery from his trips through rural England, was captivated by Turner's landscapes of the Italian countryside; and his mother suggested that the family see some of them in reality. That summer they toured Central Europe, and while walking down from the garden terrace of Schaffhausen, Ruskin's feeling for landscape became fixed; this first "sight of the Alps" was, as he pointed out many years later, "not only a revelation of the beauty of the earth, but the opening of the first page of its volume."[9]

When ill health combined with an aversion for the religious life caused him to abandon the idea of taking Holy Orders after

8. *Works*, XXXV, p. 21.
9. *Ibid.*, p. 116.

graduating from Oxford in 1842, he began to think seriously about a career in art. But what sort of career? His Evangelical background dictated a calling of high purpose, and to give his life to collecting Turners or sketching ruins smacked of dilettantism. The beauty of the natural world was good, but clearly it could not be the best. It was on the road to Norwood one afternoon while sketching a bit of ivy that the full consciousness of his vocation came to him. Suddenly he realized that "I had virtually lost all my time since I was twelve years old because no one had ever told me to draw what was really there."[10] What was "really there" in this bit of ivy and indeed in all the wonders of nature and what made them beautiful—"more [beautiful] than Gothic tracery, more than Greek vase-imagery, more than the daintiest embroiderers of the East could embroider"[11]—was the God of his Evangelical religion. The earth, he now realized, had been lent to man in order to reveal to him the laws of God and in order to increase his faith in Him. It now seemed to him that he understood the basis of his admiration for Turner: of all the English landscape painters, only Turner truly understood the truth of nature and could present that truth on canvas.

Having in effect supernaturalized his naturalism, Ruskin proceeded in *Modern Painters* to explain to his readers how the Great Architect, the Supreme Artist, put Beauty and Truth in Nature. One thing which revealed itself in every natural scene, he observed, was a mysterious infinity, an infinity of variety, not of numbers. Each tree, each flower, each cloud, while resembling others of its kind, had a distinct characteristic which made it unique. Due to this infinity in nature, no painter's hand could hope to provide a distinct representation of any object. Indeed, Ruskin felt that it was a violation of truth to give a definite representation of an object. The human eye did not see objects with any distinctness because whether a thing was placed close to the eyes or at a distance there was always some aspect of it that the individual could not see. Hence to paint with bold strokes,

10. *Ibid.*, p. 311.
11. *Ibid.*, p. 315.

to give only the general outlines as Turner was doing in his paintings, was to follow nature. Yet amid the endless variety in nature, Ruskin saw a comprehensiveness, a unity, born of physical laws which gave everything—a weedy bank, a knot of grass, a sky of clouds—a coherence, a "melodious connection of quantities" and was therefore "one of the sources of all beautiful form."[12] As he reflected on the way in which each natural scene suggested the same careful arrangement which a painter gave to organizing his canvas, he also came to believe that nature was revealing to man the Creator's government: His intelligent ordering of the world so that all things had their appointed work and place.

Having determined how the Creator put beauty into nature, it was easy enough for Ruskin to explain how Turner managed to portray this beauty on canvas: the great landscape painter had set his intelligence to the task of marshaling the infinity of nature into a harmonious whole; and, in so doing, showed how the lower pleasures, the pleasures of Nature, might lead men to God. What Turner was creating might not be perfect in its parts, Ruskin admitted, but it was near-perfect in the whole. Since this was the way in which Turner had produced his marvelous landscapes, Ruskin now thought he understood both what was required of the great artist and the artist's function in society. The artist, Ruskin argued, is a prophet, a man who could instinctively understand that "He hath made everything beautiful, in his time,"[13] and whose duty is the same as that of a preacher. He did not, however, maintain that the artist was divinely inspired; he was a "God-made great man,"[14] but not God-directed. Being a Romantic, Ruskin was quick to emphasize that it was the power of the imagination in the perceiver that made for great art. The reality of this world passed through the alembic of the artist's soul before appearing on a canvas; and it was the quality of that soul that determined the quality of the art. It was the character

12. *Works*, IV, p. 112.
13. *Works*, XXXV, p. 315.
14. *Works*, V, p. 189.

of the artist which allowed him to see the perfectness and eternal beauty of the work of God more truly and accurately than other men; and the resulting service which the great artist performed for mankind was to lift the veil and make all men see that beauty born of order.

These, then, were the aesthetic theories which Ruskin put before his readers in the pages of *Modern Painters I* and *II*. Yet, as was noted earlier, his views on art evolved over a period of years, and nowhere is this more apparent than in the first and third editions of *Modern Painters*. Whereas the first edition was certainly an original and illuminating contribution to art criticism, it did reveal the author's youth. The limited scope of the edition, with its focus on Turner as the most religious of all landscape painters, indicated Ruskin's chief deficiency as an art critic—namely, as Francis Townsend says, that "he did not know what he was talking about."[15] Although he was acquainted with the masterpieces of landscape painting in the great European museums, his knowledge of medieval and Renaissance art, as a critic of the first edition pointed out, was rather limited. Eager to supply abundant evidence for his views, Ruskin decided that, before writing *Modern Painters II*, he would study the masterpieces of Christian art; as a consequence, the revised edition of *Modern Painters I*, which we usually read, reflects a much broader knowledge of art than their author possessed at the time he began his career as an art critic.

These studies of Continental art produced unexpected results. Instead of simply furnishing additional evidence for his contentions, they posed a set of entirely new questions demanding answers if his theories were to hold together. One of his discoveries was that the art of the Italian primitives was more straightforwardly religious than the art of Turner; these medieval painters praised the Creator by painting scenes directly from the Bible,

15. Francis Townsend, *Ruskin and the Landscape Feeling* (Urbana: University of Illinois Press, 1951), p. 26. I wish to acknowledge my indebtedness to Francis Townsend for a number of the ideas presented in these paragraphs on Ruskin's development as an art critic.

not obscure landscapes. Medieval art was unmistakably religious; and if he was right in his contention that religious art served to improve the morals of the citizenry, a high moral order should result from such great religious art. Yet Ruskin did not find this to be consistently the case. Not even the colossal power of the art of Tintoretto, for example, was able to save the Venetians from sliding down to the depths of immorality.

Ruskin therefore qualified his earlier views. In his later works of art criticism, he continued to maintain both that artistic taste was a moral disposition and that virtue was a prime requisite in the soul of the painter; but he was less certain about the social and moral effects of great art. He was reduced to arguing that noble art is the product of a religious rather than an irreligious society. In *The Stones of Venice*, instead of insisting as he does in *Modern Painters* that the great artist can in a sense determine the moral character of his age, he shifts his ground and contends that the artist is molded by the age in which he lives. If the age is pagan, unspiritual, and sterile, like fifth-century Greece, it may allow an extraordinary genius like Phidias to develop his powers to the fullest, but it will force the mass of its artisans to seek a geometric perfection secured by line and rule. If the age is imitative, ignoble, and decadent, like the Renaissance, the resulting art will exhibit the dominant quality of the age. On the other hand, if the age is religious, as was thirteenth or fourteenth century Venice, the resulting art will be noble and religious. In the most important chapter of the work, "On the Nature of Gothic," he states that medieval society, instead of making a slave of the artisan by forcing him to carry out the plans of some master designer or asking the artisan to imitate slavishly the art of antiquity, recognized "in small things as well as great, the individual value of every soul."[16] Subjects which were beyond the skill of the medieval artisan could be rendered abstractly and thereby the society as well as the artisan confessed its imperfection. Those subjects which the medieval artisan could execute

16. *Works*, X, pp. 189–190.

with ease were rendered in great detail. Just as earlier Ruskin had insisted that nature achieves beauty by drawing together imperfect objects into a unified whole, he now maintained that Gothic society of the thirteenth and fourteenth centuries created beauty in architecture by receiving from each of the inferior minds that worked on its cathedrals what that mind could give and "out of fragments full of imperfection," raised the work up into a "stately and unaccusable whole."[17]

For Ruskin, then, art served as a sort of index of national wealth. If the art of a given period was great, it was because good men painted it; and living in a society which loved spiritual beauty accounted for their spiritual goodness. As Ruskin mused on these ideas while writing *The Stones of Venice*, the whole modern industrial and materialistic social order of the nineteenth century rose before him. Surveying the art of his own time, he was not able to find this sense of beauty in either the lower or higher arts, for wherever one looked there was ugliness. Along with the ugliness in art came the new economic system with its social stresses and injustices, and Ruskin connected the two. Injustice and ugliness, he wrote, proceed from the same root, with injustice coming first. Hence, if Victorian society wanted to lead a beautiful and moral life, if it wanted to be happy, it must find a way to make prominent again the social ethos which had prevailed in the Middle Ages—the last period of human happiness.

As John Rosenberg has pointed out, Ruskin recreated for his readers a Middle Ages more glorious than the reality: it became to him a "kind of second Eden, a Christianized Golden Age, a pastoral and holy paradise."[18] He praised the Middle Ages because the period was free of the iniquities that had come with the division of labor. The medieval artisan was no mere mechanic: he took pride and pleasure in his work because he was both the designer and executant. Moreover, the Middle Ages understood the true nature of freedom. Although that society was

17. *Ibid.*, p. 190.
18. John Rosenberg, *The Darkening Glass: A Portrait of Ruskin's Genius* (New York: Columbia University Press, 1961), p. 54.

hierarchical, medieval man had true liberty; he knew that "to obey another man, to labor for him, yield reverence to him or to his place, is not slavery."[19] Indeed, in Ruskin's eyes, the hierarchical structure of medieval society made for the best sort of liberty—"liberty from care."[20] But just as the Greeks had degraded their artisans by restricting their creativity to mere geometric perfection, Industrial England, he maintained, was destroying the souls of men by making them mere machines to be "numbered with its wheels, and weighed with its hammer strokes."[21]

By 1853, when the final volume of *The Stones of Venice* appeared, Ruskin had traveled a considerable distance from his original premises. In the ten years since the publication of *Modern Painters I*, the landscape feeling which had prompted his interest in art was gone, and he now called that volume "my rubbishy book."[22] Equally significant, he had almost ceased to believe in the Evangelical religion which had colored almost every page of his early work. Always an avid student of geology, he had first attended a meeting of the Geological Society in 1837; and since then the reading of geological studies had steadily increased his doubts concerning the account of creation presented in Genesis. He could do very well with "the old Evangelical formulas," he wrote his friend Henry Acland in 1851, "If only the Geologists would let me alone . . . but those dreadful Hammers! I hear the clink of them at the end of every cadence of the Bible verses."[23] And yet despite his waning faith in the old formulas, Ruskin could not accept unbelief. Writing to his father in 1848, he had declared that since the existence of God could not be proved or disproved, each man had the option to believe as he wished. Ruskin chose to believe. But the dogmatism which had marked his earlier work became less evident and his allusions

19. *Works*, X, p. 194.
20. *Ibid.*
21. *Ibid.*, p. 195.
22. *Works*, IV, p. xxvii.
23. *Works*, XXXVI, p. 115.

to the Creator in *The Stones of Venice* and the remaining volumes of *Modern Painters* stressed His mysterious incomprehensibility and His eternal laws rather than His living Presence.

Possibly due to the seriousness of the questions which were troubling his mind and the radical change in the routine of his life in the 1850's, a concern for the state of national life gradually replaced Ruskin's interest in the production of art. In 1851, he became acquainted with the greatest living transcendentalist, Thomas Carlyle, and by 1855 he was a frequent visitor at Carlyle's home in Chelsea. In Carlyle, whose *On Heroes and Hero-Worship* (1841) he had earlier dismissed as seeming to be "absolute bombast,"[24] he now found a kindred spirit, a man whose social thought corresponded closely to his own. (In fact, he confessed to Carlyle that his ideas probably appeared to be "bits of yourself spoiled."[25]) The friendship with Carlyle was not the only new experience for Ruskin in the 1850's. At the zenith of his career as an art critic, he was sought by various organizations as a lecturer, and on trips to the large industrial cities of England, he observed that the English countryside which he had found so lovely as a boy was growing uglier and that the faces of his countrymen bore the stamp of unhappiness. Moreover, taking account of the affluence and privileges that he had been born to, he began to suffer from a stricken conscience, a disorder which, as shown by *Hard Times*, was also afflicting his friend and favorite novelist, Charles Dickens. Perhaps in an effort to sooth his conscience, he joined some of the more eminent members of the Christian Socialist movement—F. D. Maurice, Thomas Hughes, and Charles Kingsley—in forming the Working Men's College. Its aim was to make available to the working classes the same kind of education enjoyed by the more privileged classes and to assist them in developing their intellectual and spiritual natures. Dutifully, Ruskin tried to provide the working men an education in art: once a week for five years he set his students to copy exactly

24. *Ibid.*, p. 25.
25. *Ibid.*, p. 184.

as they saw them such objects as white leather balls, leaves, and even trees which he had sent down to the college from his home in Denmark Hill.

The weekly meetings were a significant experience for a man who had had little contact with the working classes. They confirmed his growing feeling that capitalist civilization was a paradise for only a few. Looking back over his life, he began to wonder whether he had not given himself over to dilettantism after all, whether, under present conditions, art was a "Crime or only an Absurdity."[26] To Ruskin, it seemed increasingly futile to urge the production of great art if artists saw no beauty in the world about them, only "vegetation, dung-hills, strawyards, and all the soilings and stains of every common labour,"[27] and if the mass of mankind was so preoccupied with ekeing out a bare existence as not to be refreshed or educated by great art. Clearly the life of the working man would have to be more than drudgery before culture would have any meaning again; and if Ruskin learned any lesson from his years at the Working Men's College, it was that the life of the British laborer was absolute drudgery and degradation. As he told the Public Institutions Committee in the spring of 1860, "the labour of a day in England oppresses a man and breaks him down and it is not refreshment to him to use his mind."[28] Ruskin also informed the committee that the workman educated in the streets of English manufacturing towns could never attain a sufficient refinement of eye to produce a thing of beauty and that what he endured in the way of housing and environment tended to blunt his senses. Asked what he believed should be done to improve conditions among the poor, Ruskin said that labor should be so regulated that "it shall be impossible for men to be so entirely crushed in mind and body as they are by the system of competition."[29]

26. *Letters of John Ruskin to Charles Eliot Norton*, I, 85.
27. *Works*, V, p. 377.
28. *Works*, XVI, p. 475.
29. *Ibid.*, p. 480.

III

A few months later, when *"Unto This Last"* appeared in *Cornhill Magazine,* the contemporary press labeled as dangerous Ruskin's remarks on the economic conditions of the poor. One critic, in a manner reminiscent of the words of Dickens' Mr. Podsnap, wrote that the essays were intended to cause hatred and ingratitude among the poor and that "the sentiment that the poor are worse off than they ought to be in comparison with the rich" was socialistic.[30] While the critic mistakenly believed that Ruskin was inciting the poor to revolt, his emotionalism is understandable: to an Englishman who had lived through the riots in Kennington Common in 1848 any essays which seemed to preach economic or political reform to the poor were socially irresponsible. In this case readers probably looked upon the essays as not only irresponsible but decidedly inopportune. Englishmen were taking pride in the fact that the laborer was—economically speaking—better off in 1860 than in the hungry forties, the decade in which Carlyle wrote of England's plethoric wealth and Engels told the world that "every morning fifty thousand Londoners do not know where they will sleep at night."[31] Indeed, unparalleled prosperity had come to England, and the middle class was content to think that if this was not the best of all possible worlds, at least it was as good as man could make it.

If the workman was generally less restive in the 1850's and the 1860's than he had been a decade before, it was not because of any radical change in his situation. A great many English workers still had difficulty living under these so-called improved conditions, for prosperity had not begun to trickle down to the mass of the laborers. The skilled laborer, it is true, was living at least several notches above the poverty line. On his income of between twenty-eight and thirty-eight shillings a week he and his family

---

30. *The Saturday Review,* August 4, 1860, p. 136.
31. Friedrich Engels, *The Condition of the Working Class in England,* trans. W. O. Henderson and W. H. Chaloner (Oxford: Basil Blackwell, 1958), pp. 37–38.

could live without being haunted by the spectre of the poorhouse. But the unskilled worker, belonging to the most numerous group in the labor force, lived the life of an animal. With trade unionism among the unskilled still several years away, with no legal minimum wage laws, with few safety regulations governing the conditions under which he labored, the unskilled laborer was a helpless pawn of the industrial system. His wages were so low that he often had to be content with a diet of whelks, bean soup, and eel. The housing available to him was wretched, being usually without a water supply and sanitation facilities of any kind. Often enough a whole family occupied a single room. Seeking an escape from their wretchedness, a great many of the laborers spent their wages on drink. Ignorant, living ugly and sordid lives, performing long and excessive toil, and given to reckless improvidence, the unskilled laborer was a creature who was rapidly ceasing to be a man.

The economic system in which the unskilled laborer had to earn his wages was extremely competitive. The factories of the 1850's and 1860's, where the lot of the worker was perhaps most wretched, were small firms which sold their goods to a middle man or merchant who often enough subsidized the manufacturer whose goods were in demand. These merchants had an iron grip on foreign trade and dealt with a number of different manufacturers, playing one off against another in terms of price, quality of goods, and type of product. Since there was competition among merchants as well as among manufacturers, vicious price-cutting was the rule; and large profits were derived more from a rapid turnover of goods than from a wide margin on each particular item sold. Labor was the one factor over which the manufacturer had positive control in regulating his costs, and he found it desirable not to keep men in steady employment. In addition, many manufacturers cheated their workers out of what they did earn by truck (paying workers in commodities rather than currency) and by fining them for tardiness, whistling, and talking. The only tie between manufacturer and worker was an economic one. The employer referred to his workmen as "hands"; and the operatives felt no loyalty or sense of identity with the firm. Their aim was to get as much as they could for themselves, even if that meant underbidding the wages of their fellow-workers or bargaining simultaneously with several employers.

It was not easy to rise out of these circumstances. The workman discerning enough to recognize that he needed an advantage of some sort over his fellow-workers if he was to make himself more marketable, had few opportunities to learn a skill. The only educational opportunities available to him were in the Church and in the self-improvement institutes, such as the Mechanics Institution and Literary Institute started by Brougham and Birkbeck in the 1820's. The education offered by the Church was entirely religious. It was intended to indoctrinate permanently the working-class children with the words of the Anglican Catechism: "To order myself lowly and reverently to all my betters . . . to bear no malice nor hatred in my heart: to keep my hands from picking and stealing. . . . Not to covet nor desire other men's goods: but to learn and labor truly to get mine own living, and to do my duty in that state of life unto which it shall please God to call me." Such lessons obviously did not prepare the worker for the shops and factories of Industrial England. The Institutes, on the other hand, did attempt to teach laborers a trade, but few workmen attended them with any regularity. The lectures were too dull for tired men; and the Literary Institute books were largely white elephants.

Why was public opinion so insensitive to the plight of the laborer? To understand the psychology of those who were indifferent to these conditions, three things must be remembered. First, since these conditions were inherited from the industrial system which existed before the coming of machinery, the abuses were deep-rooted; and this made it difficult to arouse the national conscience. Second, the majority of the middle class was Evangelical; and being Evangelicals, they accepted poverty as an inevitable social fact since the Gospels told them: "For the poor always ye have with you." The factory owners were content to believe that God would provide for the diseased, mutilated, and wornout hands in their factories. Third, the minds of the English ruling classes accepted the utilitarian economic philosophy which taught that it was necessary to be cruel to the workman in order to be kind. This philosophy more than anything else determined the attitude of the age. Whereas in the eighteenth century economics had been a mere branch of moral philosophy, the seemingly self-evident truth and universality of the economic doctrines being expounded by Malthus, Ricardo, Naussau Senior, and John Stuart Mill led the Victorians to hail economics as an established science; and the writings of popularizers such as Mrs. Marcet, Archbishop Whately, and Harriet Martineau made known the doctrines of this school in an even more dogmatic and pessimistic form than they were taught by the classical economists.

This pessimism, which was unique to nineteenth-century economic thought, was rooted in the conception of nature found in the speculations of Malthus and Ricardo. Adam Smith, the founder of the school of classical economy and the author of *The Wealth of Nations* (1776), looked upon nature as the rational subject of natural science. To him, it was part of a divinely ordained, if mechanical, harmony. Ricardo and Malthus, however, saw no trace of harmony in nature. Malthus conceived of nature as hostile and niggardly, and David Ricardo, the greatest of the classical economists, saw it as blind, indifferent, and in a sense irrational. These various conceptions were united by the belief that nature is all-powerful and that man, being its subject, must live according to its laws.

Malthus believed he had discovered one of these laws in his investigation of population. In his *Essay on Population* (1798), he maintained that while the increase in organic beings is geometrical, the increase in the means of subsistence is arithmetical. He foresaw that population would eventually outrun the available supply of food and believed that the pressing need was to bring the population into a state of equilibrium. To achieve this equilibrium a decline in fertility or an increase in mortality or a combination of the two would have to occur. Malthus doubted very much that man would curb his sexual impulses, and it appeared to him that the only method of controlling the population was through misery and starvation. Since these twin terrors afflicted the laboring class more than the other classes, he concluded that it was unwise to attempt to improve their lot. As long as misery was the only check on population, improvement of any kind would only serve to increase the population and therefore increase the number of those living in misery.

Ricardo's contribution to the economic pessimism of his age was given in the form of a theory concerning wages. In his *Principles of Political Economy and Taxation* (1817), he contended that there was a "circulating capital of a large amount . . . employed in larger or smaller proportions by all the different trades of a country."[32] This capital constituted a fund out of which all wages were paid. He saw this fund (commonly referred to as "the wages fund") as continually increasing, for in his view the economic world was constantly expanding. As it expanded it necessarily pressed on the means of subsistence; and when that occurred the only remedies, according to Ricardo, were "either a reduction of people or a more rapid accumulation of capital."[33] The latter was possible in an underdeveloped country such as nineteenth-century America, but in populous England, where all available land was under cultivation, the only solution appeared to be a reduction of people. Among the classes of society, the laborer was most likely to suffer from a shortage of the means of subsistence. Unlike the landlord who owned the land and collected rent or the capitalist who ran the factories and lived off his profits, the laborer owned nothing and worked for wages which were entirely regulated by supply and demand. The laws of supply and demand, as Ricardo saw it, condemned the laborer to abject poverty. A demand for labor usually resulted in multiplying the number of workers. When the supply of workers exceeded the demand, wages fell and reduced their number. Probably Cobden provided the most succinct statement of Ri-

32. David **Ricardo**, *The Principles of Political Economy and Taxation* (New York: E. P. Dutton, 1933), p. 49.

33. *Ibid.*, p. 56.

cardo's law of supply and demand when he said that wages rose whenever two masters ran after the same man and fell whenever two men ran after the same master.

In light of these theories which seemed to the Victorians as incontrovertible and incapable of alteration by man as the laws of physics, there appeared to be little that could be done to ameliorate the conditions of the poor. Emigration, the cultivation of waste lands—these remedies might skim off a portion of the excess population for a time, but to believe that the laborer would ever be able to rear a healthy and numerous family or to taste the comforts and enjoyments of life was considered absurd. The productive resources of society, the economists argued, could be best distributed by citizens acting independently by the method of trial and error. In short, those who made the right moves in the economic jungle would destroy those who made the wrong ones. So that this law of nature could do its work, the economists, particularly the radical political group known as the Manchester school, advocated following the laissez-faire policy which would leave men free to compete with each other without any kind of interference from the State. As John Stuart Mill declared, "Every restriction of competition is an evil; every extension of it an ultimate good."[34] Competition would visit misery and suffering on a great many, but, if it could operate without any hindrance from the State, it would automatically bring with it the only kind of justice possible in this imperfect world: the strong in society would rise to their rightful place at the top of the heap and the weak would sink to the bottom.

In spite of the effect of these theories on their lives, the poor were as wedded to the idea of self-help as the rich. Classical economy, at least at the time Ruskin wrote *"Unto This Last,"* pleased nearly everyone, and it did so because it pictured life as a grand lottery with an equal chance for each ticket-holder to walk off with the stakes. Nature, operating by trial and error, might consign many to abject poverty and only a few to wealth, but it did

34. John Stuart Mill, *Principles of Political Economy*, ed. W. J. Ashley (New York: Longmans, Green, 1936), p. 793.

not say who those few might be, for in theory every man had the chance to rise to the top. Moreover, efforts to rise in society were pictured as a social good, since such actions, it was believed, invariably added to the well-being of the entire nation. The individual was encouraged to act in his own self-interest, for to act in this manner injured no one and increased the wealth of the nation and thereby benefited the entire citizenry. Every man was invited to use his powers and endowments to further himself, without considering whether there were any social or ethical restraints by which these powers should be limited. To those with money or skill—the Podsnaps, Bounderbys, and Dombeys—utilitarian economics promised virtually complete freedom for the exercise of their strength; to those without such blessings it offered the hope that they too might one day obtain the skill to be strong or the hope that, as Mr. Micawber says, "something might turn up." This economic philosophy, wedded as it was to the pleasure-pain ethics of Bentham, assured the Victorians that the individual was the most important thing in the world and that there was no standard of good and evil beyond the likes and dislikes of men. Clearly the individual was absolute; and, whether lawyer, businessman, laborer, or aristocrat, the nineteenth-century Englishman was led to believe that there were no ends of any consequence other than his ends, no laws other than his own desires, and no limits to his actions other than what he felt his fellow-beings would endure from him.

IV

Like Matthew Arnold's *Culture and Anarchy* (1869), *"Unto This Last,"* in addition to being a polemic against the principles and assumptions of the classical economists, attempts to provide an alternative to the utilitarian conception of happiness. The aim of the work, as Ruskin wrote years later in *Fors Clavigera*, is to teach "the laws of [the happy] life."[35] This assertion makes clear that Ruskin's objective is essentially the same as that of the

35. *Works,* XXIX, p. 137.

utilitarians. He shared their belief that the end of human associa-
tion is happiness; but, while he was as dedicated to achieving
this end as they were, the difference between his approach to
social reform and theirs is fundamental. The utilitarian theory
of social reform was dynamic. Taking the circumstances of society
as always changing, the utilitarians believed that men should
derive their moral principles by educing the greatest opportunities from these circumstances as they come. Their conception of
happiness, therefore, was relativistic; they felt that only by giving
human nature full freedom from all external restraints, only by
allowing society to expand and improve in all kinds of directions,
could the happiness of each individual citizen be secured. Ruskin's theory of social reform, on the other hand, was static. He
believed in an absolute, not a relativistic, norm of human happiness. Instead of welcoming the benefits wrought by the new
inventions of his day, he believed that he was living in a debased
time. The ugly and filthy cities of nineteenth-century England,
the horrible instances of human suffering and degradation reported by the newspapers, the unhappy faces of the workers of
London and Manchester, all indicated to him that material prosperity had been purchased at the price of human dignity, beauty,
and social peace. The century, like Demas, had set its heart on
this world, had chosen to follow the Prince of the World rather
than the Prince of Peace. In Ruskin's eyes, what the age needed
was not ethical experimentation, not freedom from all restraint,
but the submission of the individual will to the discipline of
objective values. "A nation which means to conduct itself wisely,"
he explains in *The Political Economy of Art* (1857), must establish authority over itself . . . which it must resolve to obey even
at times when the laws of authority appear irksome to the body
of the people or injurious to certain masses of it."[36]

For Ruskin the laws of authority by which society should govern itself are absolute and incontrovertibly true. They are not
derived from sense experience or syllogistic reasoning like the

36. *Works*, XVI, p. 25.

laws of Bentham, James Mill, or Ricardo; they are "Heaven's and Nature's."[37] Earlier, as the reader will recall, Ruskin conceived of the laws which made for the Beauty of Nature as an effluence of God; now he is affirming that the laws which should govern social intercourse are likewise spiritual laws, laws which are beyond the reach of our logical understanding and which "are not comprehensible until one begins to act on them."[38] One such law which Ruskin singles out in *Unto This Last* is the law of help which teaches men the Christian principle of helping each other, and bears witness against the saying "every man's hand against his neighbor." Another such law is the law of honesty, which, if observed, would put an end to lying and stealing in the marketplace.

There is yet another law which, although not specifically mentioned in *"Unto This Last,"* informs its social philosophy: the law of reverence. Perhaps more than the two just mentioned, it requires some explanation since it embodies Ruskin's conception of human nature and indicates what he considers the limits of self-development. Like Carlyle, Ruskin adheres to the Calvinistic idea of predestination, which leads him to label as essentially absurd the democratic notion that "every man is as good as his neighbor." As he says in *Time and Tide* (1867), there are "unconquerable differences in the clay of the human creature."[39] Accepting the fact of these differences, he believes that man's character and his capacities are irrevocably fixed at birth; while education and a good environment will help each man to realize his particular excellence and will assure that each man will reach his proper station in society, the quality of the individual soul can not be changed. It is understandable then, why Ruskin believed that society should be hierarchical and that the whole duty of each man should be to find his place in that society and give obedience and reverence to those who have superior capacities and character. As a consequence Ruskin's State provides for the

37. *Works*, XXVII, p. 276.
38. *Ibid.*
39. *Works*, XVII, p. 405.

tyranny of the wisest; slavery is not a manifestation of political oppression but "an inherent, natural, and eternal inheritance."[40]

In Ruskin's social philosophy there is one law which includes all of these spiritual laws—the law of justice. By justice, he does not mean mere legality. His conception is similar to Plato's and requires the organic ordering of the entire social order. Conceiving of justice as that virtue which must exist in the relationship between classes if the good society is to be realized, Plato in *The Republic* defines justice as each man having and doing his own: each individual in the State developing his capabilities to the fullest and doing that work for which he is best suited by capacity and education. If a just man is one who does his own business, a just state is one in which all do the work for which they are fitted without interfering with the work of other men. The effect of justice on the social order in Plato's ideal commonwealth, as in Ruskin's, is to unite the various classes of society and make their work means to a common end.

Obviously, Ruskin's idea of justice is little more than his conception of nature applied to the social order. Just as earlier in his career, he maintained that the Beauty of Nature resulted from the marshaling of an infinite number of individual and imperfect parts into a unified whole, in *"Unto This Last"* he conceives of the ideal social order as one in which an infinite number of imperfect human beings, by allowing their lives to be regulated by the guiding principles of help, reverence, honesty, and justice, can achieve the social order and harmony which in turn can produce the only real happiness possible for mankind. It is essentially an organic state, such as that which existed in the Middle Ages, which Ruskin wishes to bring into existence in nineteenth-century England. His theory of society is the antithesis to the prevailing political philosophy of both his time and ours, for his ideal State is authoritarian rather than democratic, cooperative rather than competitive, hierarchical rather than individualistic, and moral rather than political. And yet while his

40. *Ibid.*, p. 256.

theory of the ideal State is derived from his own aesthetic principles and from Plato, Ruskin does not allude to either in "*Unto This Last*," but suggests what he conceives to be the just social order by other means.

First of all, he defines Economy as "House-law" which is of course an exact translation of the Greek οἶκος + νόμος. He intends "House-law" to suggest first the idea of stewardship, the administration, management, and regulation of the house to the best possible advantage, and, second, the basic unit of society, the family, which can be viewed as a hierarchical unity made up of individual and in a sense incomplete parts. More frequently, however, he presents his conception of the just social order by drawing upon a source much more familiar to his readers—the Bible. It might seem strange that Ruskin turns to the Bible to illustrate his theory of society, since by this time he had abandoned the dogmatic basis of his faith; but despite his apostasy he remained a profoundly religious man who, although no longer convinced that the world was an effluence of God, found the Christian conception of an ordered, interdependent world aesthetically satisfying, and wished that the lives of men might be ordered as if "the bridle of man is the eye of God."[41] But what had once been a living faith now became an ideal for the secular world. While he refers to the laws of authority as "Nature's and Heaven's" law, it is probably safe to say that in "*Unto This Last*" they belong more certainly to the order of Nature than that of Heaven. In short, they are natural laws: the universal patterns of action which Plato and Aristotle envisioned as essential to man's being. What Ruskin does is to unite the Hellenic and Christian ideals of justice by using, as a rhetorical tactic, the revealed law of the Old and New Testament to establish the validity of natural law. By using this tactic, he gives his laws a needed aura of catholicity and apostolicity which allows him to deliver his comments *sub specie aeternitatis*.

The revealed law which Ruskin uses to convey his idea of a

41. *Works*, XVI, p. 28.

just social order is the Judaeo-Christian conception of righteousness. The Old Testament concept of righteousness or justice is not
simply a legalistic virtue, but a social and personal ideal which
makes possible the good life. On the social plane, it imposed on
the Hebrew the duty to fulfill his obligations to society by being
honest in commerce, paying fair wages, and helping the innocent
and unfortunate. It is thus a virtue which, as Ruskin says, can be
socially "healing (health-giving, or helping make whole or setting
at one)."[42] But the Hebrews also conceived of righteousness as
an inward quality, a right condition of the heart which made
for a healthful, wholesome, and harmonious personal life, and
one which, as Paul says, brought man his due from God. It is
righteousness in both its social and personal meaning that Ruskin
sees as a necessary virtue in men if his age is to be set aright.
Righteousness must become the national ethic as it was in the
Middle Ages, the last period of human happiness, for the happy
life depends on an ethical perfectness: "a harmony being ener-
gized under a true and reasonable acknowledgment of the place
in which we stand, of the circumstances over which we may have
control, of the relation of our powers to these and other beings
than ourselves, and of the divine laws which directly govern
both us and them."[43] It must be the aim of Political Economy,
Ruskin states in the Preface to "Unto This Last," to teach justice,
for only when men strive for righteousness can they hope to create a secularized version of Augustine's *civitas divina* where men
do not compete with one another, where social obligations super-
sede self-love, and where men understand the welfare economics
embodied in Christ's words: "I will give unto this last as unto
thee."

Righteousness, then, is the living essence of social ethics; and,
being the guiding principle, the Divine Jurisprudence, by which
men should determine social right from social wrong, it serves in
"Unto This Last" as not only the immutable and eternal norm

42. See p. 45 below.
43. *Works*, XIX, p. 171.

by which the democratic society of nineteenth-century England may be judged but also the beacon which will lead mankind back to true happiness. But while the law of justice is the essential moral backdrop in *"Unto This Last,"* it is not at stage center. Ruskin's principle aim in the work is to define the goal of human industry. This concern for the ends of human industry necessarily involves him in a discussion of the fundamental questions of political economy: what is the nature of wealth and how can we best produce, distribute, and consume it so that it assures a happy life for all. The work, however, is not simply a presentation of Ruskin's own economic philosophy. Due to the credence of utilitarianism among the Victorians, Ruskin is forced to assail the principles of his intellectual enemies in order to gain acceptance for his own economic principles. For most readers, Ruskin's references to the doctrines of classical economists, juxtaposed as they are with his own original insights, adds appreciably to the complexity of *"Unto This Last."* Therefore it is perhaps worthwhile to review the economic principles and criticism embodied in the work.

Ruskin's assault on classical economy in *"Unto This Last"* centers on two points: first, he disputes the accuracy of a number of its fundamental doctrines; second, he accuses the science of having arrogated to itself both the title and function of true political economy. He examines first what he deems are the errors of classical economy, his objective being to discredit it by demonstrating to his age the essential blindness of its theorists. In Ruskin's view, the first and fundamental error of classical economy is its conception of man's nature. Political economists, he says, base their speculations on an abstraction, the so-called "economic man." In so doing, they preach a perverted code of social action since to conceive of man as simply a "covetous machine" is to isolate him from the social affections which are a significant part of his humanity. In economic affairs, this same code isolates the individual from society by making men believe that persons are necessarily antagonistic because their interests are. As a result an economic order has emerged in which the cooperative spirit can not exist. Therefore in commercial activities, Ruskin explains, the balances of expediency or self-interest must be replaced by the "balances of justice, meaning in the term justice, to include affection—such affection as one man *owes* to another."[44]

In Ruskin's opinion a code of social action based on the balances of justice would allow the affectionate elements in human nature to come to the foreground in the industrial system, but he sees all hope of realizing such a condition blocked by another inaccuracy in classical economics, namely, the Ricardian doctrine that all relations between master and laborer must be regulated by the sovereign laws of free competition and supply and demand. Answering Ricardo, Ruskin explains that, as military and domestic service illustrate, the greatest material results are obtained when the affections are allowed to play a significant role in a man's work. Ruskin thus calls for a reorganization of labor patterned after these two forms of service which are in a sense vestiges of the medieval economic order. He states that the laborer should be paid a fixed wage and, like Carlyle, he advocates permanent rather than temporary contracts of employment. A uniform income and steady employment, he explains, would give the workmen "permanent interest in the establishment with which they are connected"[45] and thus give them a reason for doing their best. Ruskin admits that political economists do not believe that such an arrangement is possible; nevertheless some of the most important labor performed in society is paid by a fixed standard. Why then, he asks, should not the invariable standard apply to all labor?

In arguing for a uniform income and steady employment for all laborers, Ruskin is not appealing to the workmen to secure these ends through trade unionism. Like Dickens, he contends that those with the capacity for leadership and a knowledge of commercial operations, not the laborers, are obliged to produce the needed reforms. "The Roots of Honour," like the remaining essays in *"Unto This Last,"* is thus an appeal to the middle class

44. See p. 14 below.
45. See p. 19 below.

to amend the social evils which they have created. According to Ruskin, the one thing needful in commerce is the professionalization of industry, that the merchants understand and perform their proper function in the same way that the medieval guildmasters understood and performed theirs. It is Ruskin's aim to raise them up to these worthy desires, to make them govern themselves by the laws of honesty and help which, if followed, would make the professionalization of industry a reality. He informs the merchant class therefore that "In true commerce, as in true preaching or true fighting, it is necessary to admit the idea of occasional loss . . . sixpences have to be lost, as well as lives, under a sense of duty . . . the market may have its martyrdoms as well as the pulpit, and trade its heroism as well as war."[46] The merchant's business is to provide for life, and if necessary to die for it; rather than wealth, the object of his life should be to produce the best commodity at the lowest possible price and, equally important, to take a paternalistic interest in his men.

It is in the second essay, "The Veins of Wealth," that Ruskin takes up his second indictment against classical economics, namely, that it has wrongfully assumed the title and function of true political economy. To the classical theorist, Ruskin says, economics is simply the science of getting rich and the work of economists consists of formulating the laws by which riches are acquired. To Ruskin, such a science is mercantile economy, not political economy. By limiting their study of economics to the ascertainable facts of the marketplace, Ruskin contends that the economists have lost sight of the true scope of political economy: they have confused riches with wealth since by wealth they mean mere money or material possessions. As a consequence, they have narrowed and degraded the meaning of wealth and deal with riches which are largely irrelevant to the well-being of the nation since wealth is not merely economic activities and economic goods but any vital activity or useful commodity which adds to the well-being of the nation.

46. See p. 24 below.

Ruskin, however, not only condemns classical economics because its conception of wealth is narrow and irrelevant, he also reproves its apologists for their insistence on dissociating economics from ethics. Unlike Marx, whose critique of nineteenth-century orthodox economics is based on a philosophy of history, Ruskin criticizes the moral and social consequences which result from following the laws of classical economics. Despite the fact that men talk as if riches were absolute, riches, Ruskin says, is a relative term, "implying its opposite 'poor.' "[47] Since all men can not attain riches, it is clear that those who seek riches strive, not to accumulate goods, but power over labor. "Mercantile economy, the economy of 'merces' or of 'pay,' signifies the accumulation, in the hands of individuals, of legal or moral claim upon, or power over, the labour of others; every such claim implying precisely as much poverty or debt on one side, as it implies riches or right on the other."[48] The economic result of this condition is that a large portion of the labor of the nation is devoted to supplying the luxuries and personal extravagances for a class that does no work; the moral result is clearly the ownership by one individual of another. Economics as preached by the classical theorists, Ruskin concludes, is an individual science concerned with helping a select few who are trying to amass riches; and the industrial system which they have helped to create consists of a small number of plutocrats with a vast number of paupers serving them for subsistence wages.

These misconceptions about the nature and possession of wealth make it obvious to Ruskin that the economists do not know the science they preach, for in his view they have missed the central problem of economics—human welfare. Ruskin therefore calls upon his age to enlarge the scope of political economy: to analyze the divisions of the science of economics—production, consumption, distribution, and the nature of wealth—from the standpoint of social rather than individual welfare. He points out that the stress put on the production of commodities and the

47. See p. 30 below.
48. See pp. 30–31 below.

increase of productive power, two factors which orthodox economists considered attributes of a healthy economy, is meaningless unless some attention is given to what commodities are produced and how the productive power of the nation is applied. In short, for Ruskin, the true test of production lies in the consumption of goods: not any goods, however, only useful ones. In opposition to economists such as Malthus, who believed that money should be spent freely to increase the output of commodities, Ruskin insists that the nation must look to the usefulness of what it consumes and who consumes it, so that neither human nor material resources are wasted. It is perhaps worthwhile to note that Ruskin is likewise critical of one of the great shibboleths of nineteenth-century economics—the theory concerning abstinence. Wealth, Ruskin says, should not be hoarded nor left to multiply itself by interest. These practices may bring an individual commercial wealth, but they injure the nation. The true function of capital is not to be an instrument of profit but to furnish good for life by producing something different than itself. Furthermore, he advises his countrymen to bear in mind the human cost in the production of wealth. The body politic, he says, is weakened if men spend their lives manufacturing trivialities, if their employment involves excessive, monotonous, or uninteresting toil, or if their employment causes them to lose their self-respect since such labor—no matter what it adds to the income of the nation—degrades the men who perform it.

Ruskin's paternalistic view of society leads him to disagree with the views of the classical economists concerning the distribution of wealth. He rejects outright the Ricardian doctrine that the wealth of the nation is shared in rent, interest, and wages, for he sees all too clearly that under this system the laborer works so that the shareholder and the landowner may live in idleness. Although in Ruskin's social philosophy, "If a man will not work, neither shall he eat," his rejection of Ricardo's theory of distribution does not mean that he believes in the equality of wealth. What he wants clearly understood is that the rich have no more right to the property of the poor than the poor have to the property of the rich. To escape what he considers an immoral system of distribution preached by the classical economists, Ruskin insists that the wealth of the nation should be shared in accordance with the laws of justice. Hence where a Marxist would advocate "from each according to his talents, to each according to his needs," Ruskin presses for a system of distribution founded on the principle "from each according to his talents, to each according to his due." But how are we to determine what is each man's due? To give a man his due requires some evaluation of what commodities and services are to be esteemed. This problem leads Ruskin to grapple with the whole question of value, and it is his thought on this aspect of economics which represents his most important contribution to economic thought.

Value is a very difficult idea to grasp in *"Unto This Last."* Indeed it is not an easy term to comprehend in the writings of any economist, since, as W. S. Jevons has indicated, it is a very elusive word which can mean, depending on the circumstances, value in exchange, value in use, or simply that which is esteemed. The term is especially troublesome in *"Unto This Last"* because all three meanings figure into Ruskin's treatment of the subject. It is easy enough to perceive that Ruskin does not accept the meaning which the classical economists assigned to the term. In discussing value, Ricardo and Mill meant simply value in exchange, that is, what an object would bring in the marketplace. Seeking to establish an objective basis for the ratio of exchange between goods, they maintained that labor determined value: that the value of a commodity could be measured by the labor needed to produce it. In other words, the cost of production determined the necessary price or value of a commodity.

Ruskin was the first man in his age to declare that this theory of value based on cost ignored the most fundamental consideration in any discussion of value, namely, what is the actual, or human, value of a commodity. In his view, it is impossible to arrive at an objective or ethically neutral conception of value. Wealth, Mill states, consists of all useful and agreeable objects which possess exchange value; but Ruskin points out that, although having earlier discounted the importance of moral and humanistic considerations in economics, Mill does not see that without these considerations there can be no criterion of either the agreeable or the useful. According to Ruskin, what makes a commodity useful or agreeable depends on the desires and tastes of human beings. In other words, the agreeableness of an object depends on the tastes of the consumer; and taste, as Ruskin was to explain later in *The Crown of Wild Olive* (1866), "is not only a part and index of morality;—it is the ONLY morality."[49] Thus whether a person buys this commodity or that, whether he buys gin or bread, depends on his moral disposition.

Having established that value has its source not in exchange but in the capacities and dispositions of buyers, Ruskin is now ready to define value. At the outset, his definition of value seems to be nothing more than the traditional concept of value in use. The value of an object, he says, lies in its life-giving quality, its power to sustain life. However he adds to this notion of value in use or, as he refers to it, "intrinsic value" the idea of "acceptant capacity"—the merits and faculties in the possessor which make an object useful to him. Although later in his Preface to *Bibliotheca Pastorum* (1876), he claims that the idea of acceptant capacity is implied in the economics of Xenephon, in all probability the idea originates from his aesthetics, where the creation of beauty results from the interaction between the perceiver's imagination and a natural scene. For Ruskin the potentiality for good or "valor" of an object is thus always twofold: First, its intrinsic value, the absolute power of the object to support life, independent of opinion or quantity; and second, its acceptant capacity, its suitableness to the person possessing it and his vital power to use it. Yet neither intrinsic value nor acceptant capacity taken alone represent wealth. Effective wealth, as he explains in *Munera Pulveris* (1862–1863), exists "only where intrinsic value and acceptant capacity come together."[50]

49. *Works*, XVIII, p. 434.
50. *Works*, XVII, p. 154.

By including the idea of acceptant capacity in his theory of value, Ruskin helped to change the direction of nineteenth-century economics. Since acceptant capacity involves the tastes and capacities of human beings, its appearance in economic thought shifted the emphasis from the cost-oriented theory of value preached by the economists to a theory of value based on demand. To give a citizen his due, Ruskin says, we must give him in real wages, that is, commodities, those things which answer his needs and which he esteems. It is imperative therefore that men ask for the right things. Hence the essential work of political economists is not only to determine what are useful or life-giving things but also to produce the capacity to use them in the citizenry. Political economists in effect must become physicians rather than anatomists: educating men to the difference between a demand for life, which is wealth, and a demand for death, which is "illth." For to produce life—to extend it, to enrich it, to strive to help it include more than meat, indeed to help it to include salvation, wisdom, truth, and virtue should in the final analysis be the aim of all political economy, since "THERE IS NO WEALTH BUT LIFE."[51] This conception of wealth and political economy, Ruskin admits, may appear strange to readers accustomed to think of economics in terms of self-interest, supply and demand, and free competition, but in his view only a political economy founded on the laws of justice and seeking to realize the true wealth of nations can lead us forward to the golden days when "over these fields of ours the winds of Heaven shall be pure and upon them the work of men shall be done in honour and truth."[52]

LLOYD J. HUBENKA

The Creighton University

51. See p. 88 below.
52. *Works*, XXVIII, p. 427.

Selected Bibliography

COOK, E. T. *The Life of John Ruskin.* 2 vols. London: George Allen, 1911.

EVANS, JOAN. *John Ruskin.* London: Jonathan Cape, 1954.

FAIN, JOHN T. *Ruskin and the Economists.* Nashville: Vanderbilt University Press, 1956.

HOBSON, J. A. *John Ruskin, Social Reformer.* Boston: Dana Estes & Co., 1898.

HOUGH, GRAHAM. "Ruskin," in *The Last Romantics.* London: Gerald Duckworth, 1949.

LEON, DERRICK. *Ruskin: The Great Victorian.* London: Routledge & Kegan Paul, 1949.

ROSENBERG, JOHN D. *The Darkening Glass: A Portrait of Ruskin's Genius.* New York: Columbia University Press, 1961.

SHAW, BERNARD. *Ruskin's Politics.* London: The Ruskin Centenary Council, 1921; reprinted in Shaw, Bernard. *Platform and Pulpit.* Ed. by Dan H. Laurence. London: Rupert Hart-Davis, 1962.

STEPHEN, LESLIE. "John Ruskin," in *Studies of a Biographer.* Second Series, Vol. III. London: Gerald Duckworth, 1902.

TOWNSEND, FRANCIS G. *Ruskin and the Landscape Feeling.* Urbana: University of Illinois Press, 1951.

WHITEHOUSE, J. HOWARD (ED.). *Ruskin the Prophet and Other Centenary Studies.* London: Allen & Unwin, 1920.

WILENSKI, R. H. *John Ruskin: An Introduction to Further Study of His Life and Works.* London: Faber & Faber, 1933.

A Note On The Text

THIS edition reprints the text of *"Unto This Last"* from the great edition of Ruskin, *The Works of John Ruskin*, edited by E. T. Cook and Alexander Wedderburn, published in London from 1903 to 1912. Except for correcting one misprint, no intentional changes have been made in the text. Ruskin's footnotes are indicated by "(Ruskin's note)." Like anyone else who has worked with Ruskin, I am indebted to the meticulous scholarship of Cook and Wedderburn in preparing the numbered footnotes. While I shorten and modify many of their notes, my use of their material should be apparent to anyone who has used the Library Edition. With an eye to the modern student, I translate the Greek and Latin terms and phrases in the text and notes, and, as best I can, I attempt to explain some of Ruskin's more fanciful classical allusions and etymologies.

I wish to thank Reverend M. Joseph Costelloe, S.J., Department of Classics, The Creighton University, for his help with a number of Greek and Latin phrases, and Michael Sundermeier, Gordon N. Bergquist, and James Karabatsos, Department of English, The Creighton University for their kindness in reading my introduction and advising me upon it.

L. J. H.

"UNTO THIS LAST"

"Friend, I do thee no wrong. Didst not thou agree with me for a penny? Take that thine is, and go thy way. I will give unto this last even as unto thee."

"If ye think good, give me my price; and if not, forebear. So they weighed for my price thirty pieces of silver."

Author's Preface

1. The four following essays were published eighteen months ago in the *Cornhill Magazine*, and were reprobated in a violent manner, as far as I could hear, by most of the readers they met with.

Not a whit the less, I believe them to be the best, that is to say, the truest, rightest-worded, and most serviceable things I have ever written; and the last of them, having had especial pains spent on it, is probably the best I shall ever write.

"This," the reader may reply, "it might be, yet not therefore well written." Which, in no mock humility, admitting, I yet rest satisfied with the work, though with nothing else that I have done; and purposing shortly to follow out the subjects opened in these papers, as I may find leisure, I wish the introductory statements to be within the reach of any one who may care to refer to them. So I republish the essays as they appeared. One word only is changed, correcting the estimate of a weight;[1] and no word is added.[2]

2. Although, however, I find nothing to modify in these papers, it is matter of regret to me that the most startling of

1. See paragraph 48, p. 50.
2. (Ruskin's note) *Note to Second Edition.—An addition is made to the note in the Fourteenth page* of the preface of this book; which, being the most precious, in its essential contents, of all that I have ever written, I reprint word for word and page for page, after that addition, and make as accessible as I can, to all. [The second edition appeared in 1877; in this edition "the fourteenth page" is p. 6 and the note to which Ruskin refers is note 7.]

all the statements in them,—that respecting the necessity of the organization of labour, with fixed wages,—should have found its way into the first essay; it being quite one of the least important, though by no means the least certain, of the positions to be defended. The real gist of these papers, their central meaning and aim, is to give, as I believe for the first time in plain English,—it has often been incidentally given in good Greek by Plato and Xenophon, and good Latin by Cicero and Horace,[3]—a logical definition of WEALTH: such definition being absolutely needed for a basis of economical science. The most reputed essay on that subject which has appeared in modern times, after opening with the statement that "writers on political economy profess to teach, or to investigate,[4] the nature of wealth," thus follows up the declaration of its thesis—"Every one has a notion, sufficiently correct for common purposes, of what is meant by wealth." ... "It is no part of the design of this treatise to aim at metaphysical nicety of definition."[5]

3. Metaphysical nicety, we assuredly do not need; but physical nicety, and logical accuracy, with respect to a physical subject, we as assuredly do.

Suppose the subject of inquiry, instead of being House-law (*Oikonomia*), had been Star-law (*Astronomia*), and that, ignoring distinction between stars fixed and wandering, as here between wealth radiant and wealth reflective, the writer had begun thus: "Every one has a notion, sufficiently correct for common purposes, of what is meant by stars. Metaphysical nicety in the definition of a star is not the object of this treatise";—the essay so opened might yet have been far more true in its final statements, and a

3. For specific passages where Ruskin finds implied definitions of wealth in the works of these classical writers, see Plato *Laws* v. 742–743 and *The Republic* iii 416E; Horace *Satires* ii. 3. 104–110; Cicero *De Officiis* i. 42; and Xenophon *Economist* i 10–12. For Ruskin's translation of the passage from Xenephon, see note 18 to "Ad Valorem."

4. (Ruskin's note) Which? for where investigation is necessary, teaching is impossible.

5. (Ruskin's note) *Principles of Political Economy*. By J. S. Mill. Preliminary remarks, p. 2.

thousandfold more serviceable to the navigator, than any treatise on wealth, which founds its conclusions on the popular conception of wealth, can ever become to the economist.

4. It was, therefore, the first object of these following papers to give an accurate and stable definition of wealth. Their second object was to show that the acquisition of wealth was finally possible only under certain moral conditions of society, of which quite the first was a belief in the existence, and even, for practical purposes, in the attainability of honesty.

Without venturing to pronounce—since on such a matter human judgment is by no means conclusive—what is, or is not, the noblest of God's works, we may yet admit so much of Pope's assertion[6] as that an honest man is among His best works presently visible, and, as things stand, a somewhat rare one; but not an incredible or miraculous work; still less an abnormal one. Honesty is not a disturbing force, which deranges the orbits of economy; but a consistent and commanding force, by obedience to which—and by no other obedience—those orbits can continue clear of chaos.

5. It is true, I have sometimes heard Pope condemned for the lowness, instead of the height, of his standard:—"Honesty is indeed a respectable virtue; but how much higher may men attain! Shall nothing more be asked of us than that we be honest?"

For the present, good friends, nothing. It seems that in our aspirations to be more than that, we have to some extent lost sight of the propriety of being so much as that. What else we may have lost faith in, there shall be here no question; but assuredly we have lost faith in common honesty, and in the working power of it. And this faith, with the facts on which it may rest, it is quite our first business to recover and keep: not only believing, but even by experience assuring ourselves, that there are yet in the world men who can be restrained from fraud otherwise than by the fear of losing employment;[7] nay, that it is even accurately

6. *Essay on Man*, IV. 247.

7. (Ruskin's note) "The effectual discipline which is exercised over a work-

in proportion to the number of such men in any State, that the said State does or can prolong its existence.

To these two points, then, the following essays are mainly directed. The subject of the organization of labour is only casually touched upon; because, if we once can get a sufficient quantity of honesty in our captains, the organization of labour is easy, and will develop itself without quarrel or difficulty; but if we cannot get honesty in our captains, the organization of labour is for evermore impossible.

6. The several conditions of its possibility I purpose to examine at length in the sequel.[8] Yet, lest the reader should be alarmed by the hints thrown out during the following investigation of first principles, as if they were leading him into unexpectedly dangerous ground, I will, for his better assurance, state at once the worst of the political creed at which I wish him to arrive.

(1.) First,—that there should be training schools for youth established, at Government cost,[9] and under Government disci-

---

man is not that of his corporation, but of his customers. It is the fear of losing their employment which restrains his frauds, and corrects his negligence." (*Wealth of Nations*, Book I. chap. 10.)

Note to Second Edition.—The only addition I will make to the words of this book shall be a very earnest request to any Christian reader to think within himself what an entirely damned state of soul any human creature must have got into, who could read with acceptance such a sentence as this: much more, write it; and to oppose to it, the first commercial words of Venice, discovered by me in her first church:—

"Around this temple, let the Merchant's law be just, his weights true, and his contracts guileless."

If any of my present readers think that my language in this note is either intemperate, or unbecoming, I will beg them to read with attention the Eighteenth paragraph of *Sesame and Lilies;* and to be assured that I never, myself, now use, in writing, any word which is not, in my deliberate judgment, the fittest for the occasion.

Venice.

Sunday, 18th March, 1877.

8. Ruskin's intention to deal with this subject more fully is partly realized in a later work, *Munera Pulveris.*

9. (Ruskin's note) It will probably be inquired by near-sighted persons, out of what funds such schools could be supported. The expedient modes of direct

pline, over the whole country; that every child born in the country should, at the parent's wish, be permitted (and, in certain cases, be under penalty required) to pass through them; and that, in these schools, the child should (with other minor pieces of knowledge hereafter to be considered) imperatively be taught, with the best skill of teaching that the country could produce, the following three things:—

(a) The laws of health, and the exercises enjoined by them;
(b) Habits of gentleness and justice; and
(c) The calling by which he is to live.

(2.) Secondly,—that, in connection with these training schools, there should be established, also entirely under Government regulation, manufactories and workshops for the production and sale of every necessary of life, and for the exercise of every useful art. And that, interfering no whit with private enterprise, nor setting any restraints or tax on private trade, but leaving both to do their best, and beat the Government if they could,—there should, at these Government manufactories and shops, be authoritatively good and exemplary work done, and pure and true substance sold; so that a man could be sure, if he chose to pay the Government price, that he got for his money bread that was bread, ale that was ale, and work that was work.

(3.) Thirdly,—that any man, or woman, or boy, or girl, out of employment, should be at once received at the nearest Government school, and set to such work as it appeared, on trial, they were fit for, at a fixed rate of wages determinable every year;— that, being found incapable of work through ignorance, they should be taught, or being found incapable of work through sickness, should be tended; but that being found objecting to work, they should be set, under compulsion of the strictest nature,

---

provision for them I will examine hereafter; indirectly, they would be far more than self-supporting. The economy in crime alone, (quite one of the most costly articles of luxury in the modern European market,) which such schools would induce, would suffice to support them ten times over. Their economy of labour would be pure gain, and that too large to be presently calculable.

to the more painful and degrading forms of necessary toil, especially to that in mines and other places of danger (such danger being, however, diminished to the utmost by careful regulation and discipline), and the due wages of such work be retained, cost of compulsion first abstracted—to be at the workman's command, so soon as he has come to sounder mind respecting the laws of employment.

(4.) Lastly,—that for the old and destitute, comfort and home should be provided; which provision, when misfortune had been by the working of such a system sifted from guilt, would be honourable instead of disgraceful to the receiver. For (I repeat this passage out of my *Political Economy of Art*, to which the reader is referred for farther detail)[10] "a labourer serves his country with his spade, just as a man in the middle ranks of life serves it with sword, pen, or lancet. If the service be less, and, therefore, the wages during health less, then the reward when health is broken may be less, but not less honourable; and it ought to be quite as natural and straightforward a matter for a labourer to take his pension from his parish, because he has deserved well of his parish, as for a man in higher rank to take his pension from his country, because he has deserved well of his country."

To which statement, I will only add, for conclusion, respecting the discipline and pay of life and death, that, for both high and low, Livy's last words touching Valerius Publicola, *"de publico est elatus,"*[11] ought not to be a dishonourable close of epitaph.

10. *The Political Economy of Art* first appeared in 1857 and was re-issued, with additions, under the title *"A Joy for Ever"; and its Price in the Market* in 1880. The passage to which Ruskin refers in the text may be found in "Addenda, p. 195" to the original edition and in "Addenda, note 2nd, p. 27" to the later edition.

11. (Ruskin's note) P. Valerius, omnium consensu princeps belli pacisque artibus, anno post moritur; gloriâ ingenti, copiis familiaribus adeo exiguis, ut funeri sumtus deesset: de publico est elatus. Luxere matronæ ut Brutum."— Lib. ii. c. xvi. [The Latin quotation in the text may be translated "at the expense of the public." In Baker's translation, the entire passage reads: "Publius Valerius, a man universally allowed to have excelled all others in superior talents both for war and peace, full of glory, but in such slender

7. These things, then, I believe, and am about, as I find power, to explain and illustrate in their various bearings; following out also what belongs to them of collateral inquiry. Here I state them only in brief, to prevent the reader casting about in alarm for my ultimate meaning; yet requesting him, for the present, to remember, that in a science dealing with so subtle elements as those of human nature, it is only possible to answer for the final truth of principles, not for the direct success of plans: and that in the best of these last, what can be immediately accomplished is always questionable, and what can be finally accomplished, inconceivable.

DENMARK HILL,
     10*th* *May*, 1862.

.

circumstances, that he left not sufficient to defray the charges of his funeral. He was buried at the expense of the public, and the matrons went into mourning for him as they had done for Brutus." Together with L. Brutus, Publius Valerius took an active part in expelling the Tarquins from Rome and was thereupon elected consul in 509 B.C. Because of his efforts to secure liberties for the people, he was given the surname *Publicola*, "a friend of the people."]

Essay I

THE ROOTS OF HONOUR

1. AMONG the delusions which at different periods have possessed themselves of the minds of large masses of the human race,
perhaps the most curious—certainly the least creditable—is the
modern *soi-disant*[1] science of political economy, based on the
idea that an advantageous code of social action may be determined irrespectively of the influence of social affection.

Of course, as in the instances of alchemy, astrology, witchcraft,
and other such popular creeds, political economy has a plausible
idea at the root of it. "The social affections," says the economist,
"are accidental and disturbing elements in human nature; but
avarice and the desire of progress are constant elements. Let us
eliminate the inconstants, and, considering the human being
merely as a covetous machine, examine by what laws of labour,
purchase, and sale, the greatest accumulative result in wealth is
obtainable. Those laws once determined, it will be for each individual afterwards to introduce as much of the disturbing affectionate element as he chooses, and to determine for himself the
result on the new conditions supposed."

2. This would be a perfectly logical and successful method
of analysis, if the accidentals afterwards to be introduced were
of the same nature as the powers first examined. Supposing a
body in motion to be influenced by constant and inconstant

1. "self styled."

11

forces, it is usually the simplest way of examining its course to trace it first under the persistent conditions, and afterwards introduce the causes of variation. But the disturbing elements in the social problem are not of the same nature as the constant ones: they alter the essence of the creature under examination the moment they are added; they operate, not mathematically, but chemically, introducing conditions which render all our previous knowledge unavailable. We made learned experiments upon pure nitrogen, and have convinced ourselves that it is a very manageable gas: but, behold! the thing which we have practically to deal with is its chloride; and this, the moment we touch it on our established principles, sends us and our apparatus through the ceiling.

3. Observe, I neither impugn nor doubt the conclusion of the science if its terms are accepted. I am simply uninterested in them, as I should be in those of a science of gymnastics which assumed that men had no skeletons. It might be shown, on that supposition, that it would be advantageous to roll the students up into pellets, flatten them into cakes, or stretch them into cables; and that when these results were effected, the re-insertion of the skeleton would be attended with various inconveniences to their constitution. The reasoning might be admirable, the conclusions true, and the science deficient only in applicability. Modern political economy stands on a precisely similar basis. Assuming, not that the human being has no skeleton, but that it is all skeleton,[2] it founds an ossifant theory of progress on this negation of a soul; and having shown the utmost that may be made of bones, and constructed a number of interesting geometrical figures with death's-head and humeri, successfully proves the inconvenience of the reappearance of a soul among these corpuscular structures. I do not deny the truth of this theory: I simply deny its applicability to the present phase of the world.

4. This inapplicability has been curiously manifested during

2. For a probable source of the ideas found in this paragraph and the next, see Charles Dickens' article "On Strike" in *Household Words*, February 11, 1854, p. 558.

the embarrassment caused by the late strikes of our workmen.[3] Here occurs one of the simplest cases, in a pertinent and positive form, of the first vital problem which political economy has to deal with (the relation between employer and employed); and, at a severe crisis, when lives in multitudes and wealth in masses are at stake, the political economists are helpless—practically mute: no demonstrable solution of the difficulty can be given by them, such as may convince or calm the opposing parties. Obstinately the masters take one view of the matter; obstinately the operatives another; and no political science can set them at one.

5. It would be strange if it could, it being not by "science" of any kind that men were ever intended to be set at one. Disputant after disputant vainly strives to show that the interests of the masters are, or are not, antagonistic to those of the men: none of the pleaders ever seeming to remember that it does not absolutely or always follow that the persons must be antagonistic because their interests are. If there is only a crust of bread in the house, and mother and children are starving, their interests are not the same. If the mother eats it, the children want it; if the children eat it, the mother must go hungry to her work. Yet it does not necessarily follow that there will be "antagonism" between them, that they will fight for the crust, and that the mother, being strongest, will get it, and eat it. Neither, in any other case, whatever the relations of the persons may be, can it be assumed for certain that, because their interests are diverse,

3. Ruskin is probably making particular reference to the London Builders' Strike which occurred in the summer of 1859 since he registers his disapproval of the advice furnished by political economists for the settlement of that strike in a letter to E. S. Dallas, dated Sept. 4, 1859; but it is possible that he also had in mind the bitterly-contested Preston Spinners' Strike of 1854. Both strikes involved great numbers of workmen and were of long duration. The London Builders' Strike affected an estimated 90,000 workers and lasted five months; the Preston Strike concerned some 16,000 employees and dragged on for eight months. Needless to say, the duration of these strikes caused severe economic hardship to both employers and employees and had an adverse effect on the national economy.

they must necessarily regard each other with hostility, and use violence or cunning to obtain the advantage.

6. Even if this were so, and it were as just as it is convenient to consider men as actuated by no other moral influences than those which affect rats or swine, the logical conditions of the question are still indeterminable. It can never be shown generally either that the interests of master and labourer are alike, or that they are opposed; for, according to circumstances, they may be either. It is, indeed, always the interest of both that the work should be rightly done, and a just price obtained for it; but, in the division of profits, the gain of the one may or may not be the loss of the other. It is not the master's interest to pay wages so low as to leave the men sickly and depressed, nor the work-man's interest to be paid high wages if the smallness of the master's profit hinders him from enlarging his business, or con-ducting it in a safe and liberal way. A stoker ought not to desire high pay if the company is too poor to keep the engine-wheels in repair.

7. And the varieties of circumstance which influence these reciprocal interests are so endless, that all endeavour to deduce rules of action from balance of expediency is in vain. And it is meant to be in vain. For no human actions ever were intended by the Maker of men to be guided by balances of expediency, but by balances of justice. He has therefore rendered all endeavours to determine expediency futile for evermore. No man ever knew, or can know, what will be the ultimate result to himself, or to others, of any given line of conduct. But every man may know, and most of us do know, what is a just and unjust act. And all of us may know also, that the consequences of justice will be ultimately the best possible, both to others and ourselves, though we can neither say what *is* best, or how it is likely to come to pass.

I have said balances of justice, meaning, in the term justice, to include affection,—such affection as one man *owes* to another. All right relations between master and operative, and all their best interests, ultimately depend on these.

8. We shall find the best and simplest illustration of the

relations of master and operative in the position of domestic servants.

We will suppose that the master of a household desires only to get as much work out of his servants as he can, at the rate of wages he gives. He never allows them to be idle; feeds them as poorly and lodges them as ill as they will endure, and in all things pushes his requirements to the exact point beyond which he cannot go without forcing the servant to leave him. In doing this, there is no violation on his part of what is commonly called "justice." He agrees with the domestic for his whole time and service, and takes them;—the limits of hardship in treatment being fixed by the practice of other masters in his neighbourhood; that is to say, by the current rate of wages for domestic labour. If the servant can get a better place, he is free to take one, and the master can only tell what is the real market value of his labour, by requiring as much as he will give.

This is the politico-economical view of the case, according to the doctors of that science; who assert that by this procedure the greatest average of work will be obtained from the servant, and therefore the greatest benefit to the community, and through the community, by reversion, to the servant himself.

That, however, is not so. It would be so if the servant were an engine of which the motive power was steam, magnetism, gravitation, or any other agent of calculable force. But he being, on the contrary, an engine whose motive power is a Soul, the force of this very peculiar agent, as an unknown quantity, enters into all the political economist's equations, without his knowledge, and falsifies every one of their results. The largest quantity of work will not be done by this curious engine for pay, or under pressure, or by help of any kind of fuel which may be supplied by the chaldron. It will be done only when the motive force, that is to say, the will or spirit of the creature, is brought to its greatest strength by its own proper fuel: namely, by the affections.

9. It may indeed happen, and does happen often, that if the master is a man of sense and energy, a large quantity of material work may be done under mechanical pressure, enforced

by strong will and guided by wise method; also it may happen, and does happen often, that if the master is indolent and weak (however good-natured), a very small quantity of work, and that bad, may be produced by the servant's undirected strength, and contemptuous gratitude. But the universal law of the matter is that, assuming any given quantity of energy and sense in master and servant, the greatest material result obtainable by them will be, not through antagonism to each other, but through affection for each other; and that, if the master, instead of endeavouring to get as much work as possible from the servant, seeks rather to render his appointed and necessary work beneficial to him, and to forward his interests in all just and wholesome ways, the real amount of work ultimately done, or of good rendered, by the person so cared for, will indeed be the greatest possible.

Observe, I say, "of good rendered," for a servant's work is not necessarily or always the best thing he can give his master. But good of all kinds, whether in material service, in protective watchfulness of his master's interest and credit, or in joyful readiness to seize unexpected and irregular occasions of help.

Nor is this one whit less generally true because indulgence will be frequently abused, and kindness met with ingratitude. For the servant who, gently treated, is ungrateful, treated ungently, will be revengeful; and the man who is dishonest to a liberal master will be injurious to an unjust one.

10. In any case, and with any person, this unselfish treatment will produce the most effective return. Observe, I am here considering the affections wholly as a motive power; not at all as things in themselves desirable or noble, or in any other way abstractedly good. I look at them simply as an anomalous force, rendering every one of the ordinary political economist's calculations nugatory; while, even if he desired to introduce this new element into his estimates, he has no power of dealing with it; for the affections only become a true motive power when they ignore every other motive and condition of political economy. Treat the servant kindly, with the idea of turning his gratitude to account, and you will get, as you deserve, no gratitude, nor

any value for your kindness; but treat him kindly without any economical purpose, and all economical purposes will be answered; in this, as in all other matters, whosoever will save his life shall lose it, whoso loses it shall find it.[4]

11. The next clearest and simplest example of relation between master and operative is that which exists between the commander of a regiment and his men.

Supposing the officer only desires to apply the rules of discipline so as, with least trouble to himself, to make the regiment most effective, he will not be able, by any rules or administration of rules, on this selfish principle, to develop the full strength of his subordinates. If a man of sense and firmness, he may, as in the former instance, produce a better result than would be

---

4. (Ruskin's note) The difference between the two modes of treatment, and between their effective material results, may be seen very accurately by a comparison of the relations of Esther and Charlie in *Bleak House* with those of Miss Brass and the Marchioness in *Master Humphrey's Clock*.

The essential value and truth of Dickens's writings have been unwisely lost sight of by many thoughtful persons, merely because he presents his truth with some colour of caricature. Unwisely, because Dickens's caricature, though often gross, is never mistaken. Allowing for his manner of telling them, the things he tells us are always true. I wish that he could think it right to limit his brilliant exaggeration to works written only for public amusement; and when he takes up a subject of high national importance, such as that which he handled in *Hard Times*, that he would use severer and more accurate analysis. The usefulness of that work (to my mind, in several respects the greatest he has written) is with many persons seriously diminished because Mr. Bounderby is a dramatic monster, instead of a characteristic example of a worldly master; and Stephen Blackpool a dramatic perfection, instead of a characteristic example of an honest workman. But let us not lose the use of Dickens's wit and insight, because he chooses to speak in a circle of stage fire. He is entirely right in his main drift and purpose in every book he has written; and all of them, but especially *Hard Times*, should be studied with close and earnest care by persons interested in social questions. They will find much that is partial, and, because partial, apparently unjust; but if they examine all the evidence on the other side, which Dickens seems to overlook, it will appear, after all their trouble, that his view was the finally right one, grossly and sharply told. [For the source of the Biblical allusion in the text, see Matt. 10:39.]

obtained by the irregular kindness of a weak officer; but let the
sense and firmness be the same in both cases, and assuredly the
officer who has the most direct personal relations with his men,
the most care for their interests, and the most value for their
lives, will develop their effective strength, through their affection
for his own person, and trust in his character, to a degree wholly
unattainable by other means. This law applies still more string-
ently as the numbers concerned are larger: a charge may often be
successful, though the men dislike their officers; a battle has
rarely been won, unless they loved their general.

12. Passing from these simple examples to the more compli-
cated relations existing between a manufacturer and his workmen, we are met first by certain curious difficulties, resulting,
apparently, from a harder and colder state of moral elements.
It is easy to imagine an enthusiastic affection existing among
soldiers for the colonel. Not so easy to imagine an enthusiastic
affection among cotton-spinners for the proprietor of the mill.
A body of men associated for purposes of robbery (as a Highland
clan in ancient times) shall be animated by perfect affection, and
every member of it be ready to lay down his life for the life of
his chief. But a band of men associated for purposes of legal
production and accumulation is usually animated, it appears,
by no such emotions, and none of them are in any wise willing
to give his life for the life of his chief. Not only are we met by
this apparent anomaly, in moral matters, but by others connected
with it, in administration of system. For a servant or a soldier
is engaged at a definite rate of wages, for a definite period; but a
workman at a rate of wages variable according to the demand for
labour, and with the risk of being at any time thrown out of his
situation by chances of trade. Now, as, under these contingencies,
no action of the affections can take place, but only an explosive
action of *dis*affections, two points offer themselves for consideration in the matter.

The first—How far the rate of wages may be so regulated as
not to vary with the demand for labour.

The second—How far it is possible that bodies of workmen

may be engaged and maintained at such fixed rate of wages (whatever the state of trade may be), without enlarging or diminishing their number, so as to give them permanent interest in the establishment with which they are connected, like that of the domestic servants in an old family, or an *espirit de corps*, like that of the soldiers in a crack regiment.

13. The first question is, I say, how far it may be possible to fix the rate of wages, irrespectively of the demand for labour.

Perhaps one of the most curious facts in the history of human error is the denial by the common political economist of the possibility of thus regulating wages; while, for all the important, and much of the unimportant, labour, on the earth, wages are already so regulated.

We do not sell our prime-ministership by Dutch auction[5]; nor, on the decease of a bishop, whatever may be the general advantages of simony, do we (yet) offer his diocese to the clergyman who will take the episcopacy at the lowest contract. We (with exquisite sagacity of political economy!) do indeed sell commissions; but not openly, generalships: sick, we do not inquire for a physician who takes less than a guinea; litigious, we never think of reducing six-and-eightpence to four-and-sixpence; caught in a shower, we do not canvass the cabmen, to find one who values his driving at less than sixpence a mile.

It is true that in all these cases there is, and in every conceivable case there must be, ultimate reference to the presumed difficulty of the work, or number of candidates for the office. If it were thought that the labour necessary to make a good physician would be gone through by a sufficient number of students with the prospect of only half-guinea fees, public consent would soon withdraw the unnecessary half-guinea. In this ultimate sense, the price of labour is indeed always regulated by the demand for it; but, so far as the practical and immediate administration of the matter is regarded, the best labour always has been, and is, as *all* labour ought to be, paid by an invariable standard.

5. An auction in which the bidders decrease their bids until they arrive at the lowest possible price.

14. "What!" the reader perhaps answers amazedly: "pay good and bad workmen alike?"

Certainly. The difference between one prelate's sermons and his successor's—or between one physician's opinion and another's, —is far greater, as respects the qualities of mind involved, and far more important in result to you personally, than the difference between good and bad laying of bricks (though that is greater than most people suppose). Yet you pay with equal fee, contentedly, the good and bad workmen upon your soul, and the good and bad workmen upon your body; much more may you pay, contentedly, with equal fees, the good and bad workmen upon your house.

"Nay, but I choose my physician, and (?) my clergyman, thus indicating my sense of the quality of their work." By all means, also, choose your bricklayer; that is the proper reward of the good workman, to be "chosen." The natural and right system respecting all labour is, that it should be paid at a fixed rate, but the good workman employed, and the bad workman unemployed. The false, unnatural, and destructive system is when the bad workman is allowed to offer his work at half-price, and either take the place of the good, or force him by his competition to work for an inadequate sum.

15. This equality of wages, then, being the first object towards which we have to discover the directest available road, the second is, as above stated, that of maintaining constant numbers of workmen in employment, whatever may be the accidental demand for the article they produce.

I believe the sudden and extensive inequalities of demand, which necessarily arise in the mercantile operations of an active nation, constitute the only essential difficulty which has to be overcome in a just organization of labour.

The subject opens into too many branches to admit of being investigated in a paper of this kind; but the following general facts bearing on it may be noted.

The wages which enable any workman to live are necessarily higher, if his work is liable to intermission, than if it is assured and continuous; and however severe the struggle for work may become, the general law will always hold, that men must get more daily pay if, on the average, they can only calculate on work three days a week than they would require if they were sure of work six days a week. Supposing that a man cannot live on less than a shilling a day, his seven shillings he must get, either for three days' violent work, or six days' deliberate work. The tendency of all modern mercantile operations is to throw both wages and trade into the form of a lottery, and to make the workman's pay depend on intermittent exertion, and the principal's profit on dexterously used chance.

16. In what partial degree, I repeat, this may be necessary in consequence of the activities of modern trade, I do not here investigate; contenting myself with the fact that in its fatallest aspects it is assuredly unnecessary, and results merely from love of gambling on the part of the masters, and from ignorance and sensuality in the men. The masters cannot bear to let any opportunity of gain escape them, and frantically rush at every gap and breach in the walls of Fortune, raging to be rich, and affronting, with impatient covetousness, every risk of ruin, while the men prefer three days of violent labour, and three days of drunkenness, to six days of moderate work and wise rest. There is no way in which a principal, who really desires to help his workmen, may do it more effectually than by checking these disorderly habits both in himself and them; keeping his own business operations on a scale which will enable him to pursue them securely, not yielding to temptations of precarious gain; and at the same time, leading his workmen into regular habits of labour and life, either by inducing them rather to take low wages, in the form of a fixed salary, than high wages, subject to the chance of their being thrown out of work; or, if this be impossible, by discouraging the system of violent exertion for nominally high day wages, and leading the men to take lower pay for more regular labour.

In effecting any radical changes of this kind, doubtless there would be great inconvenience and loss incurred by all the originators of the movement. That which can be done with perfect convenience and without loss, is not always the thing that most needs to be done, or which we are most imperatively required to do.

17. I have already alluded to the difference hitherto existing between regiments of men associated for purposes of violence, and for purposes of manufacture; in that the former appear capable of self-sacrifice—the latter, not; which singular fact is the real reason of the general lowness of estimate in which the profession of commerce is held, as compared with that of arms. Philosophically, it does not, at first sight, appear reasonable (many writers have endeavoured to prove it unreasonable) that a peaceable and rational person, whose trade is buying and selling, should be held in less honour than an unpeaceable and often irrational person, whose trade is slaying. Nevertheless, the consent of mankind has always, in spite of the philosophers, given precedence to the soldier.

And this is right.

For the soldier's trade, verily and essentially, is not slaying, but being slain. This, without well knowing its own meaning, the world honours it for. A bravo's trade is slaying; but the world has never respected bravos more than merchants: the reason it honours the soldier is, because he holds his life at the service of the State. Reckless he may be—fond of pleasure or of adventure— all kinds of bye-motives and mean impulses may have determined the choice of his profession, and may affect (to all appearance exclusively) his daily conduct in it; but our estimate of him is based on this ultimate fact—of which we are well assured—that put him in a fortress breach, with all the pleasures of the world behind him, and only death and his duty in front of him, he will keep his face to the front; and he knows that his choice may be put to him at any moment—and has beforehand taken his part—virtually takes such part continually—does, in reality, die daily.[6]

18. Not less is the respect we pay to the lawyer and physician,

6. I Cor. 15:31.

founded ultimately on their self-sacrifice. Whatever the learning
or acuteness of a great lawyer, our chief respect for him depends
on our belief that, set in a judge's seat, he will strive to judge
justly, come of it what may. Could we suppose that he would
take bribes, and use his acuteness and legal knowledge to give
plausibility to iniquitous decisions, no degree of intellect would
win for him our respect. Nothing will win it, short of our tacit
conviction, that in all important acts of his life justice is first
with him; his own interest, second.

In the case of a physician, the ground of the honour we render
him is clearer still. Whatever his science, we would shrink from
him in horror if we found him regard his patients merely as subjects to experiment upon; much more, if we found that, receiving
bribes from persons interested in their deaths, he was using his
best skill to give poison in the mask of medicine.

Finally, the principle holds with utmost clearness as it respects
clergymen. No goodness of disposition will excuse want of science
in a physician, or of shrewdness in an advocate; but a clergyman,
even though his power of intellect be small, is respected on the
presumed ground of his unselfishness and serviceableness.

19. Now, there can be no question but that the tact, fore-
sight, decision, and other mental powers, required for the successful management of a large mercantile concern, if not such
as could be compared with those of a great lawyer, general, or
divine, would at least match the general conditions of mind
required in the subordinate officers of a ship, or of a regiment,
or in the curate of a country parish. If, therefore, all the efficient
members of the so-called liberal professions are still, somehow,
in public estimate of honour, preferred before the head of a
commercial firm, the reason must lie deeper than in the measure-
ment of their several powers of mind.

And the essential reason for such preference will be found
to lie in the fact that the merchant is presumed to act always
selfishly. His work may be very necessary to the community; but
the motive of it is understood to be wholly personal. The merchant's first object in all his dealings must be (the public believe)

to get as much for himself, and leave as little to his neighbour (or customer) as possible. Enforcing this upon him, by political statute, as the necessary principle of his action; recommending it to him on all occasions, and themselves reciprocally adopting it, proclaiming vociferously, for law of the universe, that a buyer's function is to cheapen, and a seller's to cheat,—the public, nevertheless, involuntarily condemn the man of commerce for his compliance with their own statement, and stamp him for ever as belonging to an inferior grade of human personality.

20. This they will find, eventually, they must give up doing. They must not cease to condemn selfishness; but they will have to discover a kind of commerce which is not exclusively selfish. Or, rather, they will have to discover that there never was, or can be, any other kind of commerce; that this which they have called commerce was not commerce at all, but cozening; and that a true merchant differs as much from a merchant according to laws of modern political economy, as the hero of the *Excursion* from Autolycus.[7] They will find that commerce is an occupation which gentlemen will every day see more need to engage in, rather than in the businesses of talking to men, or slaying them; that, in true commerce, as in true preaching, or true fighting, it is necessary to admit the idea of occasional voluntary loss;— that sixpences have to be lost, as well as lives, under a sense of duty; that the market may have its martyrdoms as well as the pulpit; and trade its heroisms as well as war.

May have—in the final issue, must have—and only has not had yet, because men of heroic temper have always been misguided in their youth into other fields; not recognizing what is in our days, perhaps, the most important of all fields; so that, while many a zealous person loses his life in trying to teach the form of a gospel, very few will lose a hundred pounds in showing the practice of one.

21. The fact is, that people never have had clearly explained

7. The Wanderer in Wordsworth's *The Excursion* is a peddler and a philosopher; Autolycus in Shakespeare's *The Winter's Tale* is a peddler and a rogue.

to them the true functions of a merchant with respect to other people. I should like the reader to be very clear about this.

Five great intellectual professions, relating to daily necessities of life, have hitherto existed—three exist necessarily, in every civilized nation:

The Soldier's profession is to *defend* it.

The Pastor's to *teach* it.

The Physician's to *keep it in health*.

The Lawyer's to *enforce justice* in it.

The Merchant's to *provide* for it.

And the duty of all these men is, on due occasion, to *die* for it.

"On due occasion," namely:—

The Soldier, rather than leave his post in battle.

The Physician, rather than leave his post in plague.

The Pastor, rather than teach Falsehood.

The Lawyer, rather than countenance Injustice.

The Merchant—what is *his* "due occasion" of death?

22. It is the main question for the merchant, as for all of us. For, truly, the man who does not know when to die, does not know how to live.

Observe, the merchant's function (or manufacturer's, for in the broad sense in which it is here used the word must be understood to include both) is to provide for the nation. It is no more his function to get profit for himself out of that provision than it is a clergyman's function to get his stipend. This stipend is a due and necessary adjunct, but not the object of his life, if he be a true clergyman, any more than his fee (or honorarium) is the object of life to a true physician. Neither is his fee the object of life to a true merchant. All three, if true men, have a work to be done irrespective of fee—to be done even at any cost, or for quite the contrary of fee; the pastor's function being to teach, the physician's to heal, and the merchant's, as I have said, to provide. That is to say, he has to understand to their very root the qualities of the thing he deals in, and the means of obtaining or producing it; and he has to apply all his sagacity and energy to the producing or obtaining it in perfect state, and distributing it at the cheapest possible price where it is most needed.

And because the production or obtaining of any commodity involves necessarily the agency of many lives and hands, the merchant becomes in the course of his business the master and governor of large masses of men in a more direct, though less confessed way, than a military officer or pastor; so that on him falls, in great part, the responsibility for the kind of life they lead: and it becomes his duty, not only to be always considering how to produce what he sells, in the purest and cheapest forms, but how to make the various employments involved in the production, or transference of it, most beneficial to the men employed.

23. And as into these two functions, requiring for their right exercise the highest intelligence, as well as patience, kindness, and tact, the merchant is bound to put all his energy, so for their just discharge he is bound, as soldier or physician is bound, to give up, if need be, his life, in such way as it may be demanded of him. Two main points he has in his providing function to maintain: first, his engagements (faithfulness to engagements being the real root of all possibilities, in commerce); and, secondly, the perfectness and purity of the thing provided; so that, rather than fail in any engagement, or consent to any deterioration, adulteration, or unjust and exorbitant price of that which he provides, he is bound to meet fearlessly any form of distress, poverty, or labour, which may, through maintenance of these points, come upon him.

24. Again: in his office as governor of the men employed by him, the merchant or manufacturer is invested with a distinctly paternal authority and responsibility. In most cases, a youth entering a commercial establishment is withdrawn altogether from home influence; his master must become his father, else he has, for practical and constant help, no father at hand: in all cases the master's authority, together with the general tone and atmosphere of his business, and the character of the men with whom the youth is compelled in the course of it to associate, have more immediate and pressing weight than the home influence,

and will usually neutralize it either for good or evil; so that the only means which the master has of doing justice to the men employed by him is to ask himself sternly whether he is dealing with such subordinate as he would with his own son, if compelled by circumstances to take such a position.

Supposing the captain of a frigate saw it right, or were by any chance obliged, to place his own son in the position of a common sailor: as he would then treat his son, he is bound always to treat every one of the men under him. So, also, supposing the master of a manufactory saw it right, or were by any chance obliged, to place his own son in the position of an ordinary workman; as he would then treat his son, he is bound always to treat every one of his men. This is the only effective, true, or practical RULE which can be given on this point of political economy.

And as the captain of a ship is bound to be the last man to leave his ship in case of wreck, and to share his last crust with the sailors in case of famine, so the manufacturer, in any commercial crisis or distress, is bound to take the suffering of it with his men, and even to take more of it for himself than he allows his men to feel; as a father would in a famine, shipwreck, or battle, sacrifice himself for his son.

25. All which sounds very strange: the only real strangeness in the matter being, nevertheless, that it should so sound. For all this is true, and that not partially nor theoretically, but everlastingly and practically: all other doctrine than this respecting matters political being false in premises, absurd in deduction, and impossible in practice, consistently with any progressive state of national life; all the life which we now possess as a nation showing itself in the resolute denial and scorn, by a few strong minds and faithful hearts, of the economic principles taught to our multitudes, which principles, so far as accepted, lead straight to national destruction. Respecting the modes and forms of destruction to which they lead, and, on the other hand, respecting the farther practical working of true polity, I hope to reason farther in a following paper.

Essay II

THE VEINS OF WEALTH

26. THE answer which would be made by any ordinary political economist to the statements contained in the preceding paper, is in few words as follows:—

"It is indeed true that certain advantages of a general nature may be obtained by the development of social affections. But political economists never professed, nor profess, to take advantages of a general nature into consideration. Our science is simply the science of getting rich. So far from being a fallacious or visionary one, it is found by experience to be practically effective. Persons who follow its precepts do actually become rich, and persons who disobey them become poor. Every capitalist of Europe has acquired his fortune by following the known laws of our science, and increases his capital daily by an adherence to them. It is vain to bring forward tricks of logic, against the force of accomplished facts. Every man of business knows by experience how money is made, and how it is lost."

Pardon me. Men of business do indeed know how they themselves made their money, or how, on occasion, they lost it. Playing a long-practised game, they are familiar with the chances of its cards, and can rightly explain their losses and gains. But they neither know who keeps the bank of the gambling-house, nor what other games may be played with the same cards, nor what other losses and gains, far away among the dark streets, are essentially, though invisibly, dependent on theirs in the lighted rooms. They have learned a few, and only a few, of the laws of mercantile economy; but not one of those of political economy.

27. Primarily, which is very notable and curious, I observe that men of business rarely know the meaning of the word "rich." At least, if they know, they do not in their reasonings allow for the fact, that it is a relative word, implying its opposite "poor" as positively as the word "north" implies its opposite "south." Men nearly always speak and write as if riches were absolute, and it were possible, by following certain scientific precepts, for everybody to be rich. Whereas riches are a power like that of electricity, acting only through inequalities or negations of itself. The force of the guinea you have in your pocket depends wholly on the default of a guinea in your neighbour's pocket. If he did not want it, it would be of no use to you; the degree of power it possesses depends accurately upon the need or desire he has for it,—and the art of making yourself rich, in the ordinary mercantile economist's sense, is therefore equally and necessarily the art of keeping your neighbour poor.

I would not contend in this matter (and rarely in any matter) for the acceptance of terms. But I wish the reader clearly and deeply to understand the difference between the two economies, to which the terms "Political" and "Mercantile" might not unadvisedly be attached.

28. Political economy (the economy of a State, or of citizens) consists simply in the production, preservation, and distribution, at fittest time and place, of useful or pleasurable things. The farmer who cuts his hay at the right time; the shipwright who drives his bolts well home in sound wood; the builder who lays good bricks in well-tempered mortar; the housewife who takes care of her furniture in the parlour, and guards against all waste in her kitchen; and the singer who rightly disciplines, and never overstrains her voice, are all political economists in the true and final sense: adding continually to the riches and well-being of the nation to which they belong.

But mercantile economy, the economy of "merces" or of "pay," signifies the accumulation, in the hands of individuals, of legal or moral claim upon, or power over, the labour of others; every such claim implying precisely as much poverty or debt on one side, as it implies riches or right on the other.

It does not, therefore, necessarily involve an addition to the actual property, or well-being of the State in which it exists. But since this commercial wealth, or power over labour, is nearly always convertible at once into real property, while real property is not always convertible at once into power over labour, the idea of riches among active men in civilized nations generally refers to commercial wealth; and in estimating their possessions, they rather calculate the value of their horses and fields by the number of guineas they could get for them, than the value of their guineas by the number of horses and fields they could buy with them.

29. There is, however, another reason for this habit of mind: namely, that an accumulation of real property is of little use to its owner, unless, together with it, he has commercial power over labour.[1] Thus, suppose any person to be put in possession of a large estate of fruitful land, with rich beds of gold in its gravel; countless herds of cattle in its pastures; houses, and gardens, and storehouses full of useful stores: but suppose, after all, that he could get no servants? In order that he may be able to have servants, some one in his neighbourhood must be poor, and in want of his gold—or his corn. Assume that no one is in want of either, and that no servants are to be had. He must, therefore, bake his own bread, make his own clothes, plough his own ground, and shepherd his own flocks. His gold will be as useful to him as any other yellow pebbles on his estate. His stores must rot, for he cannot consume them. He can eat no more than another man could eat, and wear no more than another man could wear. He must lead a life of severe and common labour to procure even ordinary comforts; he will be ultimately unable

1. For a possible source for the arguments advanced in this paragraph, see Aristophanes' *Plutus*, 11. 507–531, where the character Poverty maintains that, if wealth were distributed equally, servants and workmen would be impossible to obtain and insists moreover that she alone insures a supply of the goods that men covet. This play was first read by Ruskin in 1858.

to keep either houses in repair, or fields in cultivation; and forced to content himself with a poor man's portion of cottage and garden, in the midst of a desert of waste land, trampled by wild cattle, and encumbered by ruins of palaces, which he will hardly mock at himself by calling "his own."

30. The most covetous of mankind would, with small exultation, I presume, accept riches of this kind on these terms. What is really desired, under the name of riches, is, essentially, power over men; in its simplest sense, the power of obtaining for our own advantage the labour of servant, tradesman, and artist; in wider sense, authority of directing large masses of the nation to various ends (good, trivial, or hurtful, according to the mind of the rich person). And this power of wealth of course is greater or less in direct proportion to the poverty of the men over whom it is exercised, and in inverse proportion to the number of persons who are as rich as ourselves, and who are ready to give the same price for an article of which the supply is limited. If the musician is poor, he will sing for small pay, as long as there is only one person who can pay him; but if there be two or three, he will sing for the one who offers him most. And thus the power of the riches of the patron (always imperfect and doubtful, as we shall see presently even when most authoritative) depends first on the poverty of the artist, and then on the limitation of the number of equally wealthy persons, who also want seats at the concert. So that, as above stated, the art of becoming "rich," in the common sense, is not absolutely nor finally the art of accumulating much money for ourselves, but also of contriving that our neighbours shall have less. In accurate terms, it is "the art of establishing the maximum inequality in our own favour."

31. Now, the establishment of such inequality cannot be shown in the abstract to be either advantageous or disadvantageous to the body of the nation. The rash and absurd assumption that such inequalities are necessarily advantageous, lies at the root of most of the popular fallacies on the subject of political economy. For the eternal and inevitable law in this matter is, that the beneficialness of the inquality depends, first, on the

methods by which it was accomplished; and, secondly, on the purposes to which it is applied. Inequalities of wealth, unjustly established, have assuredly injured the nation in which they exist during their establishment; and, unjustly directed, injure it yet more during their existence. But inequalities of wealth, justly established, benefit the nation in the course of their establishment; and, nobly used, aid it yet more by their existence. That is to say, among every active and well-governed people, the various strength of individuals, tested by full exertion and specially applied to various need, issues in unequal, but harmonious results, receiving reward or authority according to its class and service;[2] while, in the inactive or ill-governed nation, the grada-

2. (Ruskin's note) I have been naturally asked several times with respect to the sentence in the first of these papers, "the bad workmen unemployed," "But what are you to do with your bad unemployed workmen?" Well, it seems to me the question might have occurred to you before. Your housemaid's place is vacant—you give twenty pounds a year—two girls come for it, one neatly dressed, the other dirtily; one with good recommendations, the other with none. You do not, under these circumstances, usually ask the dirty one if she will come for fifteen pounds, or twelve; and, on her consenting, take her instead of the well-recommended one. Still less do you try to beat both down by making them bid against each other, till you can hire both, one at twelve pounds a year, and the other at eight. You simply take the one fittest for the place, and send away the other, not perhaps concerning yourself quite as much as you should with the question which you now impatiently put to me, "What is to become of her?" For, all that I advise you to do, is to deal with workmen as with servants; and verily the question is of weight: "Your bad workman, idler, and rogue—what are you to do with him?"

We will consider of this presently: remember that the administration of a complete system of national commerce and industry cannot be explained in full detail within the space of twelve pages. Meantime, consider whether, there being confessedly some difficulty in dealing with rogues and idlers, it may not be advisable to produce as few of them as possible. If you examine into the history of rogues, you will find they are as truly manufactured articles as anything else, and it is just because our present system of political economy gives so large a stimulus to that manufacture that you may know it to be a false one. We had better seek for a system which will develop honest men, than for one which will deal cunningly with vagabonds. Let us reform our schools, and we shall find little reform needed in our prisons.

tions of decay and the victories of treason work out also their own rugged system of subjection and success; and substitute, for the melodious inequalities of concurrent power, the iniquitous dominances and depressions of guilt and misfortune.

32. Thus the circulation of wealth in a nation resembles that of the blood in the natural body. There is one quickness of the current which comes of cheerful emotion or wholesome exercise; and another which comes of shame or of fever. There is a flush of the body which is full of warmth and life; and another which will pass into putrefaction.

The analogy will hold down even to minute particulars. For as diseased local determination of the blood involves depression of the general health of the system, all morbid local action of riches will be found ultimately to involve a weakening of the resources of the body politic.

The mode in which this is produced may be at once understood by examining one or two instances of the development of wealth in the simplest possible circumstances.

33. Suppose two sailors cast away on an uninhabited coast, and obliged to maintain themselves there by their own labour for a series of years.

If they both kept their health, and worked steadily and in amity with each other, they might build themselves a convenient house, and in time come to possess a certain quantity of cultivated land, together with various stores laid up for future use. All these things would be real riches or property; and, supposing the men both to have worked equally hard, they would each have right to equal share or use of it. Their political economy would consist merely in careful preservation and just division of these possessions. Perhaps, however, after some time one or other might be dissatisfied with the results of their common farming; and they might in consequence agree to divide the land

---

[The sentence "the bad workmen unemployed" which is referred to in the first paragraph of the note is found in paragraph 14, p. 20 above; the question of what to do with the bad workman is discussed in paragraph 79, p. 89 below.]

they had brought under the spade into equal shares, so that each might thenceforward work in his own field, and live by it. Suppose that after this arrangement had been made, one of them were to fall ill, and be unable to work on his land at a critical time—say of sowing or harvest.

He would naturally ask the other to sow or reap for him.

Then his companion might say, with perfect justice, "I will do this additional work for you; but if I do it, you must promise to do as much for me at another time. I will count how many hours I spend on your ground, and you shall give me a written promise to work for the same number of hours on mine, whenever I need your help, and you are able to give it."

34. Suppose the disabled man's sickness to continue, and that under various circumstances, for several years, requiring the help of the other, he on each occasion gave a written pledge to work, as soon as he was able, at his companion's orders, for the same number of hours which the other had given up to him. What will the positions of the two men be when the invalid is able to resume work?

Considered as a "Polis," or state, they will be poorer than they would have been otherwise: poorer by the withdrawal of what the sick man's labour would have produced in the interval. His friend may perhaps have toiled with an energy quickened by the enlarged need, but in the end his own land and property must have suffered by the withdrawal of so much of his time and thought from them: and the united property of the two men will be certainly less than it would have been if both had remained in health and activity.

But the relations in which they stand to each other are also widely altered. The sick man has not only pledged his labour for some years, but will probably have exhausted his own share of the accumulated stores, and will be in consequence for some time dependent on the other for food, which he can only "pay" or reward him for by yet more deeply pledging his own labour.

Supposing the written promises to be held entirely valid (among civilized nations their validity is secured by legal measures[3]), the person who had hitherto worked for both might now, if he chose, rest altogether, and pass his time in idleness, not only forcing his companion to redeem all the engagements he had already entered into, but exacting from him pledges for further labour, to an arbitrary amount, for what food he had to advance to him.

35. There might not, from first to last, be the least illegality (in the ordinary sense of the word) in the arrangement; but if a stranger arrived on the coast at this advanced epoch of their political economy, he would find one man commercially Rich; the other commercially Poor. He would see, perhaps, with no small surprise, one passing his days in idleness; the other labouring for both, and living sparely, in the hope of recovering his independence at some distant period.

This is, of course, an example of one only out of many ways in which inequality of possession may be established between different persons, giving rise to the Mercantile forms of Riches and Poverty. In the instance before us, one of the men might from the first have deliberately chosen to be idle, and to put his life in pawn for present ease; or he might have mismanaged his land, and been compelled to have recourse to his neighbour for food and help, pledging his future labour for it. But what I want the reader to note especially is the fact, common to a large number of typical cases of this kind, that the establishment of the mercantile wealth which consists in a claim upon labour,

3. (Ruskin's note) The disputes which exist respecting the real nature of money arise more from the disputants examining its functions on different sides, than from any real dissent in their opinions. All money, properly so called, is an acknowledgement of debt; but as such, it may either be considered to represent the labour and property of the creditor, or the idleness and penury of the debtor. The intricacy of the question has been much increased by the (hitherto necessary) use of marketable commodities, such as gold, silver, salt, shells, etc., to give intrinsic value or security to currency; but the final and best definition of money is that it is a documentary promise ratified and guaranteed by the nation to give or find a certain quantity of labour on demand. A man's labour for a day is a better standard of value than a measure of any produce, because no produce ever maintains a consistent rate of productibility.

signifies a political diminution of the real wealth which consists in substantial possessions.

36. Take another example, more consistent with the ordinary course of affairs of trade. Suppose that three men, instead of two, formed the little isolated republic, and found themselves obliged to separate, in order to farm different pieces of land at some distance from each other along the coast: each estate furnishing a distinct kind of produce, and each more or less in need of the material raised on the other. Suppose that the third man, in order to save the time of all three, undertakes simply to superintend the transference of commodities from one farm to the other; on condition of receiving some sufficiently remunerative share of every parcel of goods conveyed, or of some other parcel received in exchange for it.

If this carrier or messenger always brings to each estate, from the other, what is chiefly wanted, at the right time, the operations of the two farmers will go on prosperously, and the largest possible result in produce, or wealth, will be attained by the little community. But suppose no intercourse between the landowners is possible, except through the travelling agent; and that, after a time, this agent, watching the course of each man's agriculture, keeps back the articles with which he has been entrusted until there comes a period of extreme necessity for them, on one side or other, and then exacts in exchange for them all that the distressed farmer can spare of other kinds of produce: it is easy to see that by ingeniously watching his opportunities, he might possess himself regularly of the greater part of the superfluous produce of the two estates, and at last, in some year of severest trial or scarcity, purchase both for himself and maintain the former proprietors thenceforward as his labourers or servants.

37. This would be a case of commercial wealth acquired on the exactest principles of modern political economy. But more distinctly even than in the former instance, it is manifest in this that the wealth of the State, or of the three men considered as a society, is collectively less than it would have been had the merchant been content with juster profit. The operations of the two

agriculturists have been cramped to the utmost; and the continual limitations of the supply of things they wanted at critical times, together with the failure of courage consequent on the prolongation of a struggle for mere existence, without any sense of permanent gain, must have seriously diminished the effective results of their labour; and the stores finally accumulated in the merchant's hands will not in any wise be of equivalent value to those which, had his dealings been honest, would have filled at once the granaries of the farmers and his own.

The whole question, therefore, respecting not only the advantage, but even the quantity, of national wealth, resolves itself finally into one of abstract justice. It is impossible to conclude, of any given mass of acquired wealth, merely by the fact of its existence, whether it signifies good or evil to the nation in the midst of which it exists. Its real value depends on the moral sign attached to it, just as sternly as that of a mathematical quantity depends on the algebraical sign attached to it. Any given accumulation of commercial wealth may be indicative, on the one hand, of faithful industries, progressive energies, and productive ingenuities: or, on the other, it may be indicative of mortal luxury, merciless tyranny, ruinous chicane. Some treasurers are heavy with human tears, as an ill-stored harvest with untimely rain; and some gold is brighter in sunshine than it is in substance.

38. And these are not, observe, merely moral or pathetic attributes of riches, which the seeker of riches may, if he chooses, despise; they are, literally and sternly, material attributes of riches, depreciating or exalting, incalculably, the monetary signification of the sum in question. One mass of money is the outcome of action which has created,—another, of action which has annihilated,—ten times as much in the gathering of it; such and such strong hands have been paralyzed, as if they had been numbed by nightshade: so many strong men's courage broken, so many productive operations hindered; this and the other false direction given to labour, and lying image of prosperity set up, on Dura plains[4] dug into seven-times-heated furnaces. That

4. Dan. 3:1.

which seems to be wealth may in verity be only the gilded index of far-reaching ruin; a wrecker's handful of coin gleaned from the beach to which he has beguiled an argosy; a camp-follower's bundle of rags unwrapped from the breasts of goodly soldiers dead; the purchase-pieces of potter's fields, wherein shall be buried together the citizen and the stranger.[5]

And therefore, the idea that directions can be given for the gaining of wealth, irrespectively of the consideration of its moral sources, or that any general and technical law of purchase and gain can be set down for national practice, is perhaps the most insolently futile of all that ever beguiled men through their vices. So far as I know, there is not in history record of anything so disgraceful to the human intellect as the modern idea that the commercial text, "Buy in the cheapest market and sell in the dearest," represents, or under any circumstances could represent, an available principle of national economy. Buy in the cheapest market?—yes; but what made your market cheap? Charcoal may be cheap among your roof timbers after a fire, and bricks may be cheap in your streets after an earthquake; but fire and earthquake may not therefore be national benefits. Sell in the dearest?—yes, truly; but what made your market dear? You sold your bread well to-day: was it to a dying man who gave his last coin for it, and will never need bread more; or to a rich man who to-morrow will buy your farm over your head; or to a soldier on his way to pillage the bank in which you have put your fortune?

None of these things you can know. One thing only you can know: namely, whether this dealing of yours is a just and faithful one, which is all you need concern yourself about respecting it; sure thus to have done your own part in bringing about ulti-mately in the world a state of things which will not issue in pillage or in death. And thus every question concerning these things merges itself ultimately in the great question of justice, which, the ground being thus far cleared for it, I will enter upon in the next paper, leaving only, in this, three final points for the reader's consideration.

5. Matt. 27:6-7.

39. It has been shown that the chief value and virtue of money consists in its having power over human beings; that, without this power, large material possessions are useless, and to any person possessing such power, comparatively unnecessary. But power over human beings is attainable by other means than by money. As I said a few pages back, the money power is always imperfect and doubtful; there are many things which cannot be reached with it, others which cannot be retained by it. Many joys may be given to men which cannot be bought for gold, and many fidelities found in them which cannot be rewarded with it.

Trite enough,—the reader thinks. Yes: but it is not so trite,— I wish it were,—that in this moral power, quite inscrutable and immeasurable though it be, there is a monetary value just as real as that respresented by more ponderous currencies. A man's hand may be full of invisible gold, and the wave of it, or the grasp, shall do more than another's with a shower of bullion. This invisible gold, also, does not necessarily diminish in spending. Political economists will do well some day to take heed of it, though they cannot take measure.

But farther. Since the essence of wealth consists in its authority over men, if the apparent or nominal wealth fail in this power, it fails in essence; in fact, ceases to be wealth at all. It does not appear lately in England, that our authority over men is absolute. The servants show some disposition to rush riotously upstairs, under an impression that their wages are not regularly paid. We should augur ill of any gentleman's property to whom this happened every other day in his drawing-room.

So, also, the power of our wealth seems limited as respects the comfort of the servants, no less than their quietude. The persons in the kitchen appear to be ill-dressed, squalid, half-starved. One cannot help imagining that the riches of the establishment must be of a very theoretical and documentary character.

40. Finally. Since the essence of wealth consists in power over men, will it not follow that the nobler and the more in number the persons are over whom it has power, the greater the wealth? Perhaps it may even appear, after some considera-

tion, that the persons themselves *are* the wealth—that these pieces
of gold with which we are in the habit of guiding them, are, in
fact, nothing more than a kind of Byzantine harness[6] or trappings,
very glittering and beautiful in barbaric sight, wherewith we
bridle the creatures; but that if these same living creatures could
be guided without the fretting and jingling of the Byzants[7] in
their mouths and ears, they might themselves be more valuable
than their bridles. In fact, it may be discovered that the true
veins of wealth are purple—and not in Rock, but in Flesh—
perhaps even that the final outcome and consummation of all
wealth is in the producing as many as possible full-breathed,
bright-eyed, and happy-hearted human creatures. Our modern
wealth, I think, has rather a tendency the other way;—most political economists appearing to consider multitudes of human
creatures not conducive to wealth,[8] or at best conducive to it
only by remaining in a dim-eyed and narrow-chested state of
being.

41. Nevertheless, it is open, I repeat, to serious question,
which I leave to the reader's pondering, whether, among national
manufactures, that of Souls of a good quality may not at last
turn out a quite leadingly lucrative one? Nay, in some far-away
and yet undreamt-of hour, I can even imagine that England may
cast all thoughts of possessive wealth back to the barbaric nations
among whom they first arose; and that, while the sands of the

6. The ornamentation on Byzantine handcraft was notably opulent and
lavish; the saddles and harnesses of Byzantine nobles sparkled with pearls,
diamonds, and cloth of gold.

7. A gold coin first struck at Constantinople. It was current in England
until superseded by the noble, a coin of Edward III.

8. A possible reference to the economic theories of Malthus and Ricardo.
Believing that population would outstrip subsistence, Malthus maintained that
the larger portion of mankind would be subjected to misery and poverty and
advocated "moral restraint" to the poor as a preventative check to population
growth. In what has come to be known as his theory of "the iron law of
wages," Ricardo asserted that the wages of workers could not rise above
the lowest level necessary for subsistence and therefore was pessimistic about
the future of the lower classes.

Indus and adamant of Golconda[9] may yet stiffen the housings of
the charger, and flash from the turban of the slave, she, as a
Christian mother, may at last attain to the virtues and the
treasures of a Heathen one, and be able to lead forth her Sons,
saying,—

"These are MY Jewels."[10]

9. The old name for Hyderabad, a ruined city in India famous for its
diamonds.
10. The well-known remark of Cornelia, mother of the Gracchi.

Essay III

QUI JUDICATIS TERRAM[1]

42. SOME centuries before the Christian era, a Jew merchant, largely engaged in business on the Gold Coast, and reported to have made one of the largest fortunes of his time (held also in repute for much practical sagacity), left among his ledgers some general maxims concerning wealth, which have been preserved, strangely enough, even to our own days. They were held in considerable respect by the most active traders of the Middle Ages, especially by the Venetians, who even went so far in their admiration as to place a statue of the old Jew on the angle of one of their principal public buildings.[2] Of late years these writings have fallen into disrepute, being opposed in every particular to the spirit of modern commerce. Nevertheless I shall reproduce a passage or two from them here, partly because they may interest the reader by their novelty; and chiefly because they will show him that it is possible for a very practical and acquisitive tradesman to hold, through a not unsuccessful career, that principle of distinction between well-gotten and ill-gotten wealth, which, partially insisted on in my last paper, it must be our work more completely to examine in this.

1. "Ye, who judge the earth." For the source of this quotation, see Wisd. of Sol. 1:1.
2. A sculpture of Solomon appears on the "Judgment Angle" of the Ducal Palace in Venice.

43

43. He says, for instance, in one place: "The getting of treasures by a lying tongue is a vanity tossed to and fro of them that seek death"[3]; adding in another, with the same meaning (he has a curious way of doubling his sayings): "Treasures of wickedness profit nothing: but justice delivers from death."[4] Both these passages are notable for their assertions of death as the only real issue and sum of attainment by any unjust scheme of wealth. If we read, instead of "lying tongue," "lying label, title, pretence, or advertisement," we shall more clearly perceive the bearing of the words on modern business. The seeking of death is a grand expression of the true course of men's toil in such business. We usually speak as if death pursued us, and we fled from him; but that is only so in rare instances. Ordinarily he masks himself—makes himself beautiful—all-glorious; not like the King's daughter, all-glorious within, but outwardly: his clothing of wrought gold. We pursue him frantically all our days, he flying or hiding from us. Our crowning success at three-score and ten is utterly and perfectly to seize, and hold him in his eternal integrity—robes, ashes, and sting.

Again: the merchant says, "He that oppresseth the poor to increase his riches, shall surely come to want."[5] And again, more strongly: "Rob not the poor because he is poor; neither oppress the afflicted in the place of business. For God shall spoil the soul of those that spoiled them."[6]

This "robbing the poor because he is poor," is especially the mercantile form of theft, consisting in taking advantage of a man's necessities in order to obtain his labour or property at a reduced price. The ordinary highwayman's opposite form of robbery—of the rich, because he is rich—does not appear to occur so often to the old merchant's mind; probably because, being less profitable and more dangerous than the robbery of the poor, it is rarely practised by persons of discretion.

3. Prov. 21:6.
4. Prov. 10:2.
5. Prov. 22:16.
6. Prov. 22:22-23.

44. But the two most remarkable passages in their deep general significance are the following:—

"The rich and the poor have met. God is their maker."[7]

"The rich and the poor have met. God is their light."[8]

They "have met": more literally, have stood in each other's way (*obviaverunt*). That is to say, as long as the world lasts, the action and counteraction of wealth and poverty, the meeting, face to face, of rich and poor, is just as appointed and necessary a law of that world as the flow of stream to sea, or the interchange of power among the electric clouds:—"God is their maker." But, also, this action may be either gentle and just, or convulsive and destructive: it may be by rage of devouring flood, or by lapse of serviceable wave;—in blackness of thunderstroke, or continual force of vital fire, soft, and shapeable into love-syllables from far away. And which of these it shall be, depends on both rich and poor knowing that God is their light; that in the mystery of human life, there is no other light than this by which they can see each other's faces, and live;—light, which is called in another of the books among which the merchant's maxims have been preserved, the "sun of justice,"[9] of which it is promised that it shall rise at last with "healing" (health-giving or helping, making whole or setting at one) in its wings. For truly

7. Wisd. of Sol. 22:2.

8. Wisd. of Sol. 29:13.

9. (Ruskin's note) More accurately, Sun of Justness; but, instead of the harsh word "Justness," the old English "Righteousness" being commonly employed, has, by getting confused with "godliness," or attracting about it various vague and broken meanings, prevented most persons from receiving the force of the passage in which it occurs. The word "righteousness" properly refers to the justice of rule, or right, as distinguished from "equity," which refers to the justice of balance. More broadly, Righteousness is King's justice; and Equity Judge's justice; the King guiding or ruling all, the Judge dividing or discerning between opposites (therefore, the double question, "Man, who made me a ruler—δικαστὴς—or a divider—μεριστὴς—over you?") Thus, with respect to the Justice of Choice (selection, the feebler and passive justice), we have from lego,—lex, legal, loi, and loyal; and with respect to the Justice of Rule (direction, the stronger and active justice), we have from rego,—rex, regal, roi, and royal. [The quotation in the note is from Luke 12:14.]

this healing is only possible by means of justice; no love, no faith, no hope will do it; men will be unwisely fond—vainly faithful,—unless primarily they are just; and the mistake of the best men through generation after generation, has been that great one of thinking to help the poor by almsgiving, and by preaching of patience or of hope, and by every other means, emollient or consolatory, except the one thing which God orders for them, justice. But this justice, with its accompanying holiness or helpfulness, being even by the best man denied in its trial time, is by the mass of men hated wherever it appears: so that, when the choice was one day fairly put to them, they denied the Helpful One and the Just;[10] and desired a murderer, sedition-raiser, and robber, to be granted to them;—the murderer instead of the Lord of Life, the sedition-raiser instead of the Prince of Peace, and the robber instead of the Just Judge of all the world.

45. I have just spoken of the flowing of streams to the sea as a partial image of the action of wealth. In one respect it is not a partial, but a perfect image. The popular economist thinks himself wise in having discovered that wealth, or the forms of property in general, must go where they are required; that where demand is, supply must follow. He farther declares that this course of demand and supply cannot be forbidden by human laws. Precisely in the same sense, and with the same certainty, the waters of the world go where they are required. Where the land falls, the water flows. The course neither of clouds nor rivers can be forbidden by human will. But the disposition and administration of them can be altered by human forethought. Whether the stream shall be a curse or a blessing, depends upon man's labour, and administering intelligence. For centuries after centuries, great districts of the world, rich in soil, and favoured in climate, have lain desert under the rage of their own rivers; nor only desert, but plague-struck. The stream which, rightly directed, would have flowed in soft irrigation from field to field—would have purified the air, given food to man and beast, and carried

10. (Ruskin's note) In another place written with the same meaning, "Just, and having salvation." [The quotation in the note is from Zech. 9:9.]

their burdens for them on its bosom—now overwhelms the plain and poisons the wind; its breath pestilence, and its work famine. In like manner this wealth "goes where it is required." No human laws can withstand its flow. They can only guide it: but this, the leading trench and limiting mound can do so thoroughly, that it shall become water of life—the riches of the hand of wisdom;[11] or, on the contrary, by leaving it to its own lawless flow, they may make it, what it has been too often, the last and deadliest of national plagues: water of Marah[12]—the water which feeds the roots of all evil.

The necessity of these laws of distribution or restraint is curiously overlooked in the ordinary political economist's definition of his own "science." He calls it, shortly, the "science of getting rich." But there are many sciences, as well as many arts, of getting rich. Poisoning people of large estates, was one employed largely in the Middle Ages; adulteration of food of people of small estates, is one employed largely now. The ancient and honourable Highland method of black mail;[13] the more modern and less honourable system of obtaining goods on credit, and the other variously improved methods of appropriation—which, in major and minor scales of industry, down to the most artistic pocket-picking, we owe to recent genius,—all come under the general head of sciences, or arts, of getting rich.

46. So that it is clear the popular economist, in calling his science the science par excellence of getting rich, must attach some peculiar ideas of limitation to its character. I hope I do not misrepresent him, by assuming that he means *his* science to be the science of "getting rich by legal or just means." In this definition, is the word "just," or "legal," finally to stand? For it

11. (Ruskin's note) "Length of days in her right hand; in her left, riches and honour." [The quotation in the note is from Prov. 3:16.]

12. Exod. 15:23.

13. In the Scottish Lowlands and in the northern counties of England during the seventeenth century, Scottish freebooters, many of whom were clansmen turned outlaw, exacted a tribute from farmers in return for immunity from robbers and raiders. Sir Walter Scott's Rob Roy is an example of such a clansman.

is possible among certain nations, or under certain rulers, or by help of certain advocates, that proceedings may be legal which are by no means just. If, therefore, we leave at last only the word "just" in that place of our definition, the insertion of this solitary and small word will make a notable difference in the grammar of our science. For then it will follow that in order to grow rich scientifically, we must grow rich justly; and, therefore, know what is just; so that our economy will no longer depend merely on prudence, but on jurisprudence—and that of divine, not human law. Which prudence is indeed of no mean order, holding itself, as it were, high in the air of heaven, and gazing for ever on the light of the sun of justice; hence the souls which have excelled in it are represented by Dante as stars forming in heaven for ever the figure of the eye of an eagle;[14] they having been in life the discerners of light from darkness; or to the whole human race, as the light of the body, which is the eye;[15] while those souls which form the wings of the bird (giving power and dominion to justice, "healing in its wings") trace also in light the inscription in heaven: "DILIGITE JUSTITIAM QUI JUDICATIS TERRAM." "Ye who judge the earth, give" (not, observe, merely love, but) "diligent love to justice": the love which seeks diligently, that is to say, choosingly, and by preference to all things else. Which judging or doing judgment in the earth is, according to their capacity and position, required not of judges only, nor of rulers only, but of all men:[16] a truth sorrowfully lost sight of even by those

14. *Paradiso*, XVIII.

15. Matt. 6:22.

16. (Ruskin's note) I hear that several of our lawyers have been greatly amused by the statement in the first of these papers that a lawyer's function was to do justice. I did not intend it for a jest; nevertheless it will be seen that in the above passage neither the determination nor doing of justice are contemplated as functions wholly peculiar to the lawyer. Possibly, the more our standing armies, whether of soldiers, pastors, or legislators (the generic term "pastor" including all teachers, and the generic term "lawyer" including makers as well as interpreters of law), can be superseded by the force of national heroism, wisdom, and honesty, the better it may be for the nation. [Ruskin discusses "a lawyer's function" in paragraph 21, p. 25.]

who are ready enough to apply to themselves passages in which
Christian men are spoken of as called to be "saints" (*i.e.,* to helpful or healing functions); and "chosen to be kings"[17] (*i.e.,* to
knowing or directing functions); the true meaning of these titles
having been long lost through the pretences of unhelpful and
unable persons to saintly and kingly character; also through the
once popular idea that both the sanctity and royalty are to
consist in wearing long robes and high crowns, instead of in
mercy and judgment;[18] whereas all true sanctity is saving power,
as all true royalty is ruling power; and injustice is part and
parcel of the denial of such power, which "makes men as the
creeping things, as the fishes of the sea, that have no ruler over
them."[19]

47. Absolute justice is indeed no more attainable than absolute truth; but the righteous man is distinguished from the
unrighteous by his desire and hope of justice, as the true man
from the false by his desire and hope of truth. And though
absolute justice be unattainable, as much justice as we need
for all practical use is attainable by all those who make it their
aim.

We have to examine, then, in the subject before us, what
are the laws of justice respecting payment of labour—no small
part, these, of the foundations of all jurisprudence.

I reduced, in my last paper, the idea of money payment to
its simplest or radical terms. In those terms its nature, and the
conditions of justice respecting it, can be best ascertained.

Money payment, as there stated, consists radically in a promise to some person working for us, that for the time and labour
he spends in our service to-day we will give or procure equiva-

17. Rom. 1:7; see also Rev. 1:6.
18. Ps. 101:1.
19. (Ruskin's note) It being the privilege of the fishes, as it is of rats and
wolves, to live by the laws of demand and supply; but the distinction of
humanity, to live by those of right. [The quotation in the text is from Hab.
1:14.]

lent time and labour in his service at any future time when he may demand it.[20]

If we promise to give him less labour than he has given us, we under-pay him. If we promise to give him more labour than he has given us, we over-pay him. In practice, according to the laws of demand and supply, when two men are ready to do the work, and only one man wants to have it done, the two men underbid each other for it; and the one who gets it to do, is under-paid. But when two men want the work done, and there is only one man ready to do it, the two men who want it done overbid each other, and the workman is over-paid.

48. I will examine these two points of injustice in succession; but first I wish the reader to clearly understand the central principle, lying between the two, of right or just payment.

When we ask a service of any man, he may either give it us freely, or demand payment for it. Respecting free gift of service, there is no question at present, that being a matter of affection—not of traffic. But if he demand payment for it, and we wish to treat him with absolute equity, it is evident that this equity can only consist in giving time for time, strength for strength, and skill for skill. If a man works an hour for us, and we only promise to work half an hour for him in return, we obtain an unjust advantage. If, on the contrary, we promise to work an hour and a half for him in return, he has an unjust advantage. The justice consists in absolute exchange; or, if there be any respect to the stations of the parties, it will not be in favour of the employer: there is certainly no equitable reason in

20. (Ruskin's note) It might appear at first that the market price of labour expressed such an exchange: but this is a fallacy, for the market price is the momentary price of the kind of labour required, but the just price is its equivalent of the productive labour of mankind. This difference will be analyzed in its place. It must be noted also that I speak here only of the exchangeable value of labour, not of that of commodities. The exchangeable value of a commodity is that of the labour required to produce it, multiplied into the force of the demand for it. If the value of the labour $= x$ and the force of demand $= y$, the exchangeable value of the commodity is xy, in which if either $x = 0$, or $y = 0$, $xy = 0$.

a man's being poor, that if he give me a pound of bread to-day, I should return him less than a pound of bread to-morrow; or any equitable reason in a man's being uneducated, that if he uses a certain quantity of skill and knowledge in my service, I should use a less quantity of skill and knowledge in his. Perhaps, ultimately, it may appear desirable, or, to say the least, gracious, that I should give in return somewhat more than I received. But at present, we are concerned on the law of justice only, which is that of perfect and accurate exchange;—one circumstance only interfering with the simplicity of this radical idea of just payment—that inasmuch as labour (rightly directed) is fruitful just as seed is, the fruit (or "interest," as it is called) of the labour first given, or "advanced," ought to be taken into account, and balanced by an additional quantity of labour in the subsequent repayment. Supposing the repayment to take place at the end of the year, or of any other given time, this calculation could be approximately made, but as money (that is to say, cash) payment involves no reference to time (it being optional with the person paid to spend what he receives at once or after any number of years), we can only assume, generally, that some slight advantage must in equity be allowed to the person who advances the labour, so that the typical form of bargain will be: If you give me an hour to-day, I will give you an hour and five minutes on demand. If you give me a pound of bread to-day, I will give you seventeen[21] ounces on demand, and so on. All that is necessary for the reader to note is, that the amount returned is at least in equity not to be *less* than the amount given.

The abstract idea, then, of just or due wages, as respects the labourer, is that they will consist in a sum of money which will at any time procure for him at least as much labour as he has given, rather more than less. And this equity or justice of payment is, observe, wholly independent of any reference to the number of men who are willing to do the work. I want a horse-

21. In *Cornhill Magazine*, the sentence read "thirteen" rather than "seventeen" ounces. See Ruskin's reference to this change in paragraph 1, of his Preface above.

shoe for my horse. Twenty smiths, or twenty thousand smiths, may be ready to forge it; their number does not in one atom's weight affect the question of the equitable payment of the one who *does* forge it. It costs him a quarter of an hour of his life, and so much skill and strength of arm, to make that horseshoe for me. Then at some future time I am bound in equity to give a quarter of an hour, and some minutes more, of my life (or of some other person's at my disposal), and also as much strength of arm and skill, and a little more, in making or doing what the smith may have need of.

49. Such being the abstract theory of just remunerative payment, its application is practically modified by the fact that the order for labour, given in payment, is general, while the labour received is special. The current coin or document is practically an order on the nation for so much work of any kind; and this universal applicability to immediate need renders it so much more valuable than special labour can be, that an order for a less quantity of this general toil will always be accepted as a just equivalent for a greater quantity of special toil. Any given craftsman will always be willing to give an hour of his own work in order to receive command over half an hour, or even much less, of national work. This source of uncertainty, together with the difficulty of determining the monetary value of skill,[22] render

22. (Ruskin's note) Under the term "skill" I mean to include the united force of experience, intellect, and passion, in their operation on manual labour: and under the term "passion" to include the entire range and agency of the moral feelings; from the simple patience and gentleness of mind which will give continuity and fineness to the touch, or enable one person to work without fatigue, and with good effect, twice as long as another, up to the qualities of character which render science possible—(the retardation of science by envy is one of the most tremendous losses in the economy of the present century)—and to the incommunicable emotion and imagination which are the first and mightiest sources of all value in art.

It is highly singular that political economists should not yet have perceived, if not the moral, at least the passionate element, to be an inextricable quantity in every calculation. I cannot conceive, for instance, how it was possible that Mr. Mill should have followed the true clue so far as to write,— "No limit can be set to the importance—even in a purely productive and

the ascertainment (even approximate) of the proper wages of any given labour in terms of a currency, matter of considerable complexity. But they do not affect the principle of exchange. The worth of the work may not be easily known; but it *has* a worth, just as fixed and real as the specific gravity of a substance, though such specific gravity may not be easily ascertainable when the substance is united with many others. Nor is there so much difficulty or chance in determining it, as in determining the ordinary maxima and minima of vulgar political economy. There are few bargains in which the buyer can ascertain with anything like precision that the seller would have taken no less;—or the seller acquire more than a comfortable faith that the purchaser would have given no more. This impossibility of precise knowledge prevents neither from striving to attain the desired point of greatest vexation and injury to the other, nor from accepting it for a scientific principle that he is to buy for the least and sell for the most possible, though what the real least or most may be he cannot tell. In like manner, a just person lays it down for a scientific principle that he is to pay a just price, and, without

---

material point of view—of mere thought," without seeing that it was logically necessary to add also, "and of mere feeling." And this the more, because in his first definition of labour he includes in the idea of it "all feelings of a disagreeable kind connected with the employment of one's thoughts in a particular occupation." True; but why not also, "feelings of an agreeable kind"? It can hardly be supposed that the feelings which retard labour are more essentially a part of the labour than those which accelerate it. The first are paid for as pain, the second as power. The workman is merely indemnified for the first; but the second both produce a part of the exchangeable value of the work, and materially increase its actual quantity.

"Fritz is with us. *He* is worth fifty thousand men." Truly, a large addition to the material force;—consisting, however, be it observed, not more in operations carried on in Fritz's head, than in operations carried on in his armies' heart. "No limit can be set to the importance of *mere* thought." Perhaps not! Nay, suppose some day it should turn out that "mere" thought was in itself a recommendable object of production, and that all Material production was only a step towards this more precious Immaterial one? [For the source of Mill's "first definition of labor," see *Principles of Political Economy*, Bk. I, chap. i, paragraph 1. The second quotation is from Bk. I, chap. ii, paragraph 8.]

being able precisely to ascertain the limits of such a price, will nevertheless strive to attain the closest possible approximation to them. A practically serviceable approximation he *can* obtain. It is easier to determine scientifically what a man ought to have for his work, than what his necessities will compel him to take for it. His necessities can only be ascertained by empirical, but his due by analytical, investigation. In the one case, you try your answer to the sum like a puzzled schoolboy—till you find one that fits; in the other, you bring out your result within certain limits, by process of calculation.

50. Supposing, then, the just wages of any quantity of given labour to have been ascertained, let us examine the first results of just and unjust payment, when in favour of the purchaser or employer: *i.e.*, when two men are ready to do the work, and only one wants to have it done.

The unjust purchaser forces the two to bid against each other till he has reduced their demand to its lowest terms. Let us assume that the lowest bidder offers to do the work at half its just price.

The purchaser employs him, and does not employ the other. The first or *apparent* result is, therefore, that one of the two men is left out of employ, or to starvation, just as definitely as by the just procedure of giving fair price to the best workman. The various writers who endeavoured to invalidate the positions of my first paper never saw this, and assumed that the unjust hirer employed *both*. He employs both no more than the just hirer. The only difference (in the outset) is that the just man pays sufficiently, the unjust man insufficiently, for the labour of the single person employed.

I say, "in the outset"; for this first or apparent difference is not the actual difference. By the unjust procedure, half the proper price of the work is left in the hands of the employer. This enables him to hire another man at the same unjust rate, on some other kind of work; and the final result is that he has two men working for him at half-price, and two are out of employ.

51. By the just procedure, the whole price of the first piece of work goes into the hands of the man who does it. No surplus being left in the employer's hands, *he* cannot hire another man for another piece of labour. But by precisely so much as his power is diminished, the hired workman's power is increased: that is to say, by the additional half of the price he has received; which additional half *he* has the power of using to employ another man in *his* service. I will suppose, for the moment, the least favourable, though quite probable, case—that, though justly treated himself, he yet will act unjustly to his subordinate; and hire at half-price if he can. The final result will then be, that one man works for the employer, at just price; one for the workman, at half-price; and two, as in the first case, are still out of employ. These two, as I said before, are out of employ in *both* cases. The difference between the just and unjust procedure does not lie in the number of men hired, but in the price paid to them, and the *persons by whom* it is paid. The essential difference, that which I want the reader to see clearly, is, that in the unjust case, two men work for one, the first hirer. In the just case, one man works for the first hirer, one for the person hired, and so on, down or up through the various grades of service; the influence being carried forward by justice, and arrested by injustice. The universal and constant action of justice in this matter is therefore to diminish the power of wealth, in the hands of one individual, over masses of men, and to distribute it through a chain of men. The actual power exerted by the wealth is the same in both cases; but by injustice it is put all into one man's hands, so that he directs at once and with equal force the labour of a circle of men about him; by the just procedure, he is permitted to touch the nearest only, through whom, with diminished force, modified by new minds, the energy of the wealth passes on to others, and so till it exhausts itself.

52. The immediate operation of justice in this respect is therefore to diminish the power of wealth, first, in acquisition of luxury, and secondly, in exercise of moral influence. The employer cannot concentrate so multitudinous labour on his own

interests, nor can he subdue so multitudinous mind to his own will. But the secondary operation of justice is not less important. The insufficient payment of the group of men working for one, places each under a maximum of difficulty in rising above his position. The tendency of the system is to check advancement. But the sufficient or just payment, distributed through a descending series of offices or grades of labour,[23] gives each subordinated person fair and sufficient means of rising in the social scale, if he chooses to use them; and thus not only diminishes the immediate power of wealth, but removes the worst disabilities of poverty.

53. It is on this vital problem that the entire destiny of the labourer is ultimately dependent. Many minor interests may sometimes appear to interfere with it, but all branch from it. For instance, considerable agitation is often caused in the minds of the lower classes when they discover the share which they nominally, and to all appearance, actually, pay out of their

23. (Ruskin's note) I am sorry to lose time by answering, however curtly, the equivocations of the writers who sought to obscure the instances given of regulated labour in the first of these papers, by confusing kinds, ranks, and quantities of labour with its qualities. I never said that a colonel should have the same pay as a private, nor a bishop the same pay as a curate. Neither did I say that more work ought to be paid as less work (so that the curate of a parish of two thousand souls should have no more than the curate of a parish of five hundred). But I said that, so far as you employ it at all, bad work should be paid no less than good work; as a bad clergyman yet takes his tithes, a bad physician takes his fee, and a bad lawyer his costs. And this, as will be farther shown in the conclusion, I said, and say, partly because the best work never was, nor ever will be, done for money at all; but chiefly because, the moment people know they have to pay the bad and good alike, they will try to discern the one from the other, and not use the bad. A sagacious writer in the *Scotsman* asks me if I should like any common scribbler to be paid by Messrs. Smith, Elder and Co. as their good authors are. I should, if they employed him—but would seriously recommend them, for the scribbler's sake as well as their own, *not* to employ him. The quantity of its money which the country at present invests in scribbling is not, in the outcome of it, economically spent; and even the highly ingenious person to whom this question occurred, might perhaps have been more beneficially employed than in printing it. [The review in the *Scotsman*, an Edinburgh daily, appeared on Aug. 9, 1860.]

wages in taxation (I believe thirty-five or forty per cent).[24] This sounds very grievous; but in reality the labourer does not pay it, but his employer. If the workman had not to pay it, his wages would be less by just that sum; competition would still reduce them to the lowest rate at which life was possible. Similarly the lower orders agitated for the repeal of the corn laws,[25] thinking they would be better off if bread were cheaper; never perceiving that as soon as bread was permanently cheaper, wages would permanently fall in precisely that proportion. The corn

24. Ruskin is referring to the total taxation which is derived from the wages of workmen and not to the share of their wages which they pay in taxation.

25. (Ruskin's note) I have to acknowledge an interesting communication on the subject of free trade from Paisley (for a short letter from "A Well-wisher" at——, my thanks are yet more due). But the Scottish writer will, I fear, be disagreeably surprised to hear, that I am, and always have been, an utterly fearless and unscrupulous free-trader. Seven years ago, speaking of the various signs of infancy in the European mind (*Stones of Venice*, vol. iii., p. 168), I wrote: "The first principles of commerce were acknowledged by the English parliament only a few months ago, in its free-trade measures, and are still so little understood by the million, that *no nation dares to abolish its custom-houses.*"

It will be observed that I do not admit even the idea of reciprocity. Let other nations, if they like, keep their ports shut; every wise nation will throw its own open. It is not the opening them, but a sudden, inconsiderate, and blunderingly experimental manner of opening them, which does harm. If you have been protecting a manufacture for a long series of years, you must not take the protection off in a moment, so as to throw every one of its operatives at once out of employ, any more than you must take all its wrappings off a feeble child at once in cold weather, though the cumber of them may have been radically injuring its health. Little by little, you must restore it to freedom and to air.

Most people's minds are in curious confusion on the subject of free-trade, because they suppose it to imply enlarged competition. On the contrary, free-trade puts an end to all competition. "Protection" (among various other mischievous functions) endeavours to enable one country to compete with another in the production of an article at a disadvantage. When trade is entirely free, no country can be competed with in the articles for the production of which it is naturally calculated; nor can it compete with any other, in the production of articles for which it is not naturally calculated. Tuscany, for instance, cannot compete with England in steel, nor England with Tuscany in oil. They

laws were rightly repealed;[26] not, however, because they directly
oppressed the poor, but because they indirectly oppressed them
in causing a large quantity of their labour to be consumed
unproductively. So also unnecessary taxation oppresses them,
through destruction of capital; but the destiny of the poor depends primarily always on this one question of dueness of wages.
Their distress (irrespectively of that caused by sloth, minor
error, or crime) arises on the grand scale from the two reacting
forces of competition and oppression. There is not yet, nor will
yet for ages be, any real over-population in the world; but a local
over-population, or, more accurately, a degree of population
locally unmanageable under existing circumstances for want of
fore-thought and sufficient machinery, necessarily shows itself
by pressure of competition; and the taking advantage of this
competition by the purchaser to obtain their labour unjustly
cheap, consummates at once their suffering and his own; for in
this (as I believe in every other kind of slavery) the oppressor
suffers at last more than the oppressed, and those magnificent
lines of Pope, even in all their force, fall short of the truth:—

> "Yet, to be just to these poor men of pelf,
>   Each does but HATE HIS NEIGHBOUR AS HIMSELF:
>   Damned to the mines, an equal fate betides
>   The slave that digs it, and the slave that hides."[27]

---

must exchange their steel and oil. Which exchange should be as frank and
free as honesty and the sea-winds can make it. Competition, indeed, arises at
first, and sharply, in order to prove which is strongest in any given manufacture possible to both; this point once ascertained, competition is at an end.
[In the Cook and Wedderburn edition, the quotation from *Stones of Venice*
is found in Vol. XI, p. 198.]

26. Enacted in 1815, the Corn Laws were intended to revive farming at a
time when the Industrial Revolution was turning England towards manufacturing. A sliding scale, introduced in 1828 and modified in 1842, supported
the price of corn (wheat and other cereal grains) by imposing a graduated
tariff on foreign grain. The Corn Laws made food expensive and aroused the
resentment of the lower classes. Following a campaign by the Anti-Corn Law
League, they were repealed by Parliament in 1846.

27. *Moral Essays*, III. 107–110.

54. The collateral and reversionary operations of justice in this matter I shall examine hereafter[28] (it being needful first to define the nature of value); proceeding then to consider within what practical terms a juster system may be established; and ultimately the vexed question of the destinies of the unemployed workmen.[29] Lest, however, the reader should be alarmed at some of the issues to which our investigations seem to be tending, as if in their bearing against the power of wealth they had something in common with those of socialism, I wish him to know, in accurate terms, one or two of the main points which I have in view.

Whether socialism has made more progress among the army and navy (where payment is made on my principles), or among

28. Ruskin does not treat of this topic within the pages of "Unto This Last." See the editor's introduction, page vii above, for a discussion of the circumstances surrounding the termination of these essays.

29. (Ruskin's note) I should be glad if the reader would first clear the ground for himself so far as to determine whether the difficulty lies in getting the work or getting the pay for it. Does he consider occupation itself to be an expensive luxury, difficult of attainment, of which too little is to be found in the world? or is it rather that, while in the enjoyment even of the most athletic delight, men must nevertheless be maintained, and this maintenance is not always forthcoming? We must be clear on this head before going farther, as most people are loosely in the habit of talking of the difficulty of "finding employment." Is it employment that we want to find, or support during employment? Is it idleness we wish to put an end to, or hunger? We have to take up both questions in succession, only not both at the same time. No doubt that work *is* a luxury, and a very great one. It is, indeed, at once a luxury and a necessity; no man can retain either health of mind or body without it. So profoundly do I feel this, that, as will be seen in the sequel, one of the principal objects I would recommend to benevolent and practical persons, is to induce rich people to seek for a larger quantity of this luxury than they at present possess. Nevertheless, it appears by experience that even this healthiest of pleasures may be indulged in to excess, and that human beings are just as liable to surfeit of labour as to surfeit of meat; so that, as on the one hand, it may be charitable to provide, for some people, lighter dinner, and more work,—for others, it may be equally expedient to provide lighter work, and more dinner. [Ruskin did not write the "sequel" that he mentions in the note; however his lecture entitled "Work" in *Crown of Wild Olive* is a lengthy discussion of the need for useful work.]

the manufacturing operatives (who are paid on my opponents' principles), I leave it to those opponents to ascertain and declare. Whatever their conclusion may be, I think it necessary to answer for myself only this: that if there be any one point insisted on throughout my works more frequently than another, that one point is the impossibility of Equality. My continual aim has been to show the eternal superiority of some men to others, sometimes even of one man to all others; and to show also the advisability of appointing such persons or person to guide, to lead, or on occasion even to compel and subdue, their inferiors according to their own better knowledge and wiser will. My principles of Political Economy were all involved in a single phrase spoken three years ago at Manchester: "Soldiers of the Ploughshare as well as Soldiers of the Sword":[30] and they were all summed in a single sentence in the last volume of *Modern Painters*—"Government and co-operation are in all things the Laws of Life; Anarchy and competition the Laws of Death."[31]

And with respect to the mode in which these general principles affect the secure possession of property, so far am I from invalidating such security, that the whole gist of these papers will be found ultimately to aim at an extension in its range; and whereas it has long been known and declared that the poor have no right to the property of the rich, I wish it also to be known and declared that the rich have no right to the property of the poor.

55. But that the working of the system which I have undertaken to develop would in many ways shorten the apparent and direct, though not the unseen and collateral, power, both of wealth, as the Lady of Pleasure, and of capital as the Lord of

30. Ruskin is referring to a lecture which he delivered at Manchester, July 10, 1857. This lecture and one given three days later on July 13 were collected and published under the title *The Political Economy of Art* and later were re-issued under the title *A Joy for Ever*. The quotation is from paragraph 15. Ruskin also quotes from *A Joy for Ever* in the Preface above, see paragraph 6, p. 8.

31. See Part VIII, chap. i.

Toil, I do not deny: on the contrary, I affirm it in all joyfulness; knowing that the attraction of riches is already too strong, as their authority is already too weighty, for the reason of mankind. I said in my last paper[32] that nothing in history had ever been so disgraceful to human intellect as the acceptance among us of the common doctrines of political economy as a science. I have many grounds for saying this, but one of the chief may be given in few words. I know no previous instance in history of a nation's establishing a systematic disobedience to the first principles of its professed religion. The writings which we (verbally) esteem as divine, not only denounce the love of money as the source of all evil,[33] and as an idolatry abhorred of the Deity, but declare mammon service to be the accurate and irreconcileable opposite of God's service: and, whenever they speak of riches absolute, and poverty absolute, declare woe to the rich, and blessing to the poor. Whereupon we forthwith investigate a science of becoming rich, as the shortest road to national prosperity.

> "Tai Cristian dannerà l'Etiòpe,
> Quando si partiranno i due collegi,
> L'UNO IN ETERNO RICCO, E L'ALTRO INÒPE."[34]

---

32. Ruskin is probably referring to his discussion of the science of political economy in paragraph 1, p. 11 above.

33. I Tim. 6:10.

34. *Paradiso*, XIX. In Cary's translation, the lines are rendered as follows:

> "Christians like these the Æthiop shall condemn,
> When that the two assemblages shall part,
> One rich eternally, the other poor."

Essay IV

AD VALOREM

56. IN the last paper we saw that just payment of labour consisted in a sum of money which would approximately obtain equivalent labour at a future time: we have now to examine the means of obtaining such equivalence. Which question involves the definition of Value, Wealth, Price, and Produce.

None of these terms are yet defined so as to be understood by the public. But the last, Produce, which one might have thought the clearest of all, is, in use, the most ambiguous; and the examination of the kind of ambiguity attendant on its present employment will best open the way to our work.

In his chapter on Capital,[1] Mr. J. S. Mill instances, as a capitalist, a hardware manufacturer, who, having intended to spend a certain portion of the proceeds of his business in buying plate and jewels, changes his mind, and "pays it as wages to additional workpeople." The effect is stated by Mr. Mill to be, that "more food is appropriated to the consumption of productive labourers."

57. Now I do not ask, though, had I written this paragraph, it would surely have been asked of me, What is to become of the silversmiths? If they are truly unproductive persons, we will acquiesce in their extinction. And though in another part of

1. (Ruskin's note) Book I. chap. iv. s. 1. To save space, my future references to Mr. Mill's work will be by numerals only, as in this instance, I. iv. 1. Ed. in 2 vols. 8vo, Parker, 1848.

the same passage, the hardware merchant is supposed also to dispense with a number of servants, whose "food is thus set free for productive purposes," I do not inquire what will be the effect, painful or otherwise, upon the servants, of this emancipation of their food. But I very seriously inquire why ironware is produce, and silverware is not? That the merchant consumes the one, and sells the other, certainly does not constitute the difference, unless it can be shown (which, indeed, I perceive it to be becoming daily more and more the aim of tradesmen to show) that commodities are made to be sold, and not to be consumed. The merchant is an agent of conveyance to the consumer in one case, and is himself the consumer in the other:[2] but the labourers are in either case equally productive, since they have produced goods to the same value, if the hardware and the plate are both goods.

And what distinction separates them? It is indeed possible that in the "comparative estimate of the moralist," with which Mr. Mill says political economy has nothing to do (III. i. 2), a steel fork might appear a more substantial production than a silver one; we may grant also that knives, no less than forks, are good produce; and scythes and ploughshares serviceable articles. But, how of bayonets? Supposing the hardware merchant to effect large sales of *these*, by help of the "setting free" of the food of his servants and his silversmith,—is he still employing productive

2. (Ruskin's note) If Mr. Mill had wished to show the difference in result between consumption and sale, he should have represented the hardware merchant as consuming his own goods instead of selling them; similarly, the silver merchant as consuming his own goods instead of selling them. Had he done this, he would have made his position clearer, though less tenable; and perhaps this was the position he really intended to take, tacitly involving his theory, elsewhere stated, and shown in the sequel of this paper to be false, that demand for commodities is not demand for labour. But by the most diligent scrutiny of the paragraph now under examination, I cannot determine whether it is a fallacy pure and simple, or the half of one fallacy supported by the whole of a greater one; so that I treat it here on the kinder assumption that it is one fallacy only. [For a further discussion of the proposition that "a demand for commodities is not a demand for labour," see paragraph 76, p. 86 below. The source of the proposition is Mill's *Principles of Political Economy*, Bk. I, chap. v, paragraph 9.]

labourers, or, in Mr. Mill's words, labourers who increase "the stock of permanent means of enjoyment" (I. iii. 4)? Or if, instead of bayonets, he supply bombs, will not the absolute and final "enjoyment" of even these energetically productive articles (each of which costs ten pounds[3]) be dependent on a proper choice of time and place for their *enfantement*; choice, that is to say, depending on those philosophical considerations with which political economy has nothing to do?[4]

58. I should have regretted the need of pointing out inconsistency in any portion of Mr. Mill's work, had not the value of his work proceeded from its inconsistencies. He deserves honour among economists by inadvertently disclaiming the principles which he states, and tacitly introducing the moral considerations with which he declares his science has no connection. Many of his chapters are, therefore, true and valuable; and the only conclusions of his which I have to dispute are those which follow from his premises.

Thus, the idea which lies at the root of the passage we have just been examining, namely, that labour applied to produce luxuries will not support so many persons as labour applied to produce useful articles, is entirely true; but the instance given fails—and in four directions of failure at once—because Mr. Mill has not defined the real meaning of usefulness. The definition which he has given—"capacity to satisfy a desire, or serve a purpose" (III. i. 2)—applies equally to the iron and silver; while the true definition—which he has not given, but which nevertheless underlies the false verbal definition in his mind, and comes out

3. (Ruskin's note) I take Mr. Helps' estimate in his essay on War. [See *Friends in Council*, New Series, 1859.]

4. (Ruskin's note) Also, when the wrought silver vases of Spain were dashed to fragments by our custom-house officers because bullion might be imported free of duty, but not brains, was the axe that broke them productive?—the artist who wrought them unproductive? Or again. If the woodman's axe is productive, is the executioner's? as also, if the hemp of a cable be productive, does not the productiveness of hemp in a halter depend on its moral more than on its material application?

once or twice by accident (as in the words "any support to life or strength" in I. iii. 5)—applies to some articles of iron, but not to others, and to some articles of silver, but not to others. It applies to ploughs, but not to bayonets; and to forks, but not to filigree.[5]

59. The eliciting of the true definitions will give us the reply to our first question, "What is value?" respecting which, however, we must first hear the popular statements.

"The word 'value,' when used without adjunct, always means, in political economy, value in exchange" (Mill, III. i. 2). So that, if two ships cannot exchange their rudders, their rudders are, in politico-economic language, of no value to either.

But "the subject of political economy is wealth."—(Preliminary remarks, page 1.)

And wealth "consists of all useful and agreeable objects which possess exchangeable value."—(Preliminary remarks, page 10.)

It appears, then, according to Mr. Mill, that usefulness and agreeableness underlie the exchange value, and must be ascertained to exist in the thing, before we can esteem it an object of wealth.

Now, the economical usefulness of a thing depends not merely on its own nature, but on the number of people who can and will use it. A horse is useless, and therefore unsaleable, if no one can ride,—a sword, if no one can strike, and meat, if no one can eat. Thus every material utility depends on its relative human capacity.

Similarly: The agreeableness of a thing depends not merely on its own likeableness, but on the number of people who can be got to like it. The relative agreeableness, and therefore saleableness of "a pot of the smallest ale," and of "Adonis painted by a running brook," depends virtually on the opinion of Demos, in the shape of Christopher Sly.[6] That is to say, the agreeableness

5. (Ruskin's note) Filigree; that is to say, generally, ornament dependent on complexity, not on art.

6. Christopher Sly is a drunken tinker who appears in the induction to Shakespeare's *The Taming of the Shrew.*

of a thing depends on its relatively human disposition.[7] Therefore, political economy, being a science of wealth, must be a
science respecting human capacities and dispositions. But moral
considerations have nothing to do with political economy (III.
i. 2). Therefore, moral considerations have nothing to do with
human capacities and dispositions.

60. I do not wholly like the look of this conclusion from Mr.
Mill's statements:—let us try Mr. Ricardo's.

"Utility is not the measure of exchangeable value, though it
is absolutely essential to it."—(Chap. I., sect. i.)[8] Essential in what
degree, Mr. Ricardo? There may be greater and less degrees of
utility. Meat, for instance, may be so good as to be fit for any
one to eat, or so bad as to be fit for no one to eat. What is the
exact degree of goodness which is "essential" to its exchangeable
value, but not "the measure" of it? How good must the meat be,
in order to possess any exchangeable value? and how bad must it
be—(I wish this were a settled question in London markets)—in
order to possess none?

There appears to be some hitch, I think, in the working even

7. (Ruskin's note) These statements sound crude in their brevity; but will
be found of the utmost importance when they are developed. Thus, in the
above instance, economists have never perceived that disposition to buy is a
wholly *moral* element in demand: that is to say, when you give a man half a
crown, it depends on his disposition whether he is rich or poor with it—
whether he will buy disease, ruin, and hatred, or buy health, advancement,
and domestic love. And thus the agreeableness or exchange value of every
offered commodity depends on production, not merely of the commodity, but
of buyers of it; therefore on the education of buyers, and on all the moral
elements by which their disposition to buy this, or that, is formed. I will
illustrate and expand into final consequences every one of these definitions
in its place: at present they can only be given with extremest brevity; for in
order to put the subject at once in a connected form before the reader, I have
thrown into one, the opening definitions of four chapters: namely, of that
on Value ("Ad Valorem"); on Price ("Thirty Pieces"); on Production ("Deme-
ter"); and on Economy ("The Law of the House"). [In the last sentence of
the note, Ruskin is again making reference to the intended continuation of
these papers; see the editor's introduction, p. vii above.]

8. *Principles of Political Economy and Taxation* (London, 1817).

of Mr. Ricardo's principles; but let him take his own example. "Suppose that in the early stages of society the bows and arrows of the hunter were of equal value with the implements of the fisherman. Under such circumstances the value of the deer, the produce of the hunter's day's labour, would be *exactly*" (italics mine) "equal to the value of the fish, the product of the fisherman's day's labour. The comparative value of the fish and game would be *entirely* regulated by the quantity of labour realized in each." (Ricardo, chap. iii. On Value.)[9]

Indeed! Therefore, if the fisherman catches one sprat, and the huntsman one deer, one sprat will be equal in value to one deer; but if the fisherman catches no sprat and the huntsman two deer, no sprat will be equal in value to two deer?

Nay; but—Mr. Ricardo's supporters may say—he means, on an average;—if the average product of a day's work of fisher and hunter be one fish and one deer, the one fish will always be equal in value to the one deer.

Might I inquire the species of fish? Whale? or whitebait?[10]

9. Ruskin's reference is somewhat misleading. Actually the quotation is from section iii of chapter I, "On Value."

10. (Ruskin's note) Perhaps it may be said, in farther support of Mr. Ricardo, that he meant, "when the utility is constant or given, the price varies as the quantity of labour." If he meant this, he should have said it; but, had he meant it, he could have hardly missed the necessary result, that utility would be one measure of price (which he expressly denies it to be); and that, to prove saleableness, he had to prove a given quantity of utility, as well as a given quantity of labour; to wit, in his own instance, that the deer and fish would each feed the same number of men, for the same number of days, with equal pleasure to their palates. The fact is, he did not know what he meant himself. The general idea which he had derived from commercial experience, without being able to analyze it, was that when the demand is constant, the price varies as the quantity of labour required for production; or, using the formula I gave in last paper—when y is constant, xy varies as x. But demand never is nor can be ultimately constant, if x varies distinctly; for, as price rises, consumers fall away; and as soon as there is a monopoly (and all scarcity is a form of monopoly, so that every commodity is affected occasionally by some colour of monopoly), y becomes the most influential condition of the price. Thus the price of a painting depends less on its merit than on the interest taken in it by the public; the price of singing less on the labour of

It would be waste of time to pursue these fallacies farther; we will seek for a true definition.

61. Much store has been set for centuries upon the use of our English classical education. It were to be wished that our well-educated merchants recalled to mind always this much of their Latin schooling,—that the nominative of *valorem* (a word already sufficiently familiar to them) is *valor*; a word which, therefore, ought to be familiar to them. *Valor*, from *valere*, to be well or strong (ὑγιαίνω);—strong, *in* life (if a man), or valiant; strong, *for* life (if a thing), or valuable. To be "valuable," therefore, is to "avail towards life." A truly valuable or availing thing is that which leads to life with its whole strength. In proportion as it does not lead to life, or as its strength is broken, it is less valuable; in proportion as it leads away from life, it is unvaluable or malignant.

The value of a thing, therefore, is independent of opinion, and of quantity. Think what you will of it, gain how much you may of it, the value of the thing itself is neither greater nor less. For ever it avails, or avails not; no estimate can raise, no disdain repress, the power which it holds from the Maker of things and of men.

the singer than the number of persons who desire to hear him; and the price of gold less on the scarcity which affects it in common with cerium or iridium, than on the sunlight colour and unalterable purity by which it attracts the admiration and answers the trust of mankind.

It must be kept in mind, however, that I use the word "demand" in a somewhat different sense from economists usually. They mean by it "the quantity of a thing sold." I mean by it "the force of the buyer's capable intention to buy." In good English, a person's "demand" signifies, not what he gets, but what he asks for.

Economists also do not notice that objects are not valued by absolute bulk or weight, but by such bulk and weight as is necessary to bring them into use. They say, for instance, that water bears no price in the market. It is true that a cupful does not, but a lake does; just as a handful of dust does not, but an acre does. And were it possible to make even the possession of a cupful or handful permanent (*i.e.*, to find a place for them), the earth and sea would be bought up by handfuls and cupfuls. [For the formula mentioned in the note, see note 20 to the last essay.]

The real science of political economy, which has yet to be distinguished from the bastard science, as medicine from witch-craft, and astronomy from astrology, is that which teaches nations to desire and labour for the things that lead to life: and which teaches them to scorn and destroy the things that lead to destruction. And if, in a state of infancy, they supposed indifferent things, such as excrescences of shell-fish, and pieces of blue and red stone, to be valuable, and spent large measures of the labour which ought to be employed for the extension and ennobling of life, in diving or digging for them, and cutting them into various shapes,—or if, in the same state of infancy, they imagine precious and beneficent things, such as air, light, and cleanliness, to be valueless,—or if, finally, they imagine the conditions of their own existence, by which alone they can truly possess or use anything, such, for instance, as peace, trust, and love, to be prudently exchangeable, when the markets offer, for gold, iron, or excrescences of shells—the great and only science of Political Economy teaches them, in all these cases, what is vanity, and what substance; and how the service of Death, the Lord of Waste, and of eternal emptiness, differs from the service of Wisdom, the Lady of Saving, and of eternal fulness; she who has said, "I will cause those that love me to inherit SUBSTANCE; and I will FILL their treasures."[11]

The "Lady of Saving," in a profounder sense than that of the savings bank, though that is a good one: Madonna della Salute,[12] —Lady of Health,—which, though commonly spoken of as if separate from wealth, is indeed a part of wealth. This word, "wealth," it will be remembered, is the next we have to define.

62. "To be wealthy," says Mr. Mill, "is to have a large stock of useful articles."[13]

I accept this definition. Only let us perfectly understand it. My opponents often lament my not giving them enough logic: I fear I must at present use a little more than they will like; but

11. Prov. 8:21.
12. The name of a famous church in Venice.
13. *Principles of Political Economy* (London, 1848), p. 8.

this business of Political Economy is no light one, and we must allow no loose terms in it.

We have, therefore, to ascertain in the above definition, first, what is the meaning of "having," or the nature of Possession. Then what is the meaning of "useful," or the nature of Utility.

And first of possession. At the crossing of the transepts of Milan Cathedral has lain, for three hundred years, the embalmed body of St. Carlo Borromeo. It holds a golden crosier, and has a cross of emeralds on its breast. Admitting the crosier and emeralds to be useful articles, is the body to be considered as "having" them? Do they, in the politico-economical sense of property, belong to it? If not, and if we may, therefore, conclude generally that a dead body cannot possess property, what degree and period of animation in the body will render possession possible?

As thus: lately in a wreck of a Californian ship, one of the passengers fastened a belt about him with two hundred pounds of gold in it, with which he was found afterwards at the bottom. Now, as he was sinking—had he the gold? or had the gold him?[14]

And if, instead of sinking him in the sea by its weight, the gold had struck him on the forehead, and thereby caused incurable disease—suppose palsy or insanity,—would the gold in that case have been more a "possession" than in the first? Without pressing the inquiry up through instances of gradually increasing vital power over the gold (which I will, however, give, if they are asked for), I presume the reader will see that possession, or "having," is not an absolute, but a gradated, power; and consists not only in the quantity or nature of the thing possessed, but also (and in a greater degree) in its suitableness to the person possessing it and in his vital power to use it.

And our definition of Wealth, expanded, becomes: "The possession of useful articles, *which we can use*." This is a very serious change. For wealth, instead of depending merely on a "have," is thus seen to depend on a "can." Gladiator's death, on a "habet"; but soldier's victory, and State's salvation, on a "quo plurimum

14. (Ruskin's note) Compare George Herbert, *The Church Porch*, Stanza 28.

posset." (Liv. VII. 6.)[15] And what we reasoned of only as accumulation of material, is seen to demand also accumulation of capacity.

63. So much for our verb. Next for our adjective. What is the meaning of "useful"?

The inquiry is closely connected with the last. For what is capable of use in the hands of some persons, is capable, in the hands of others, of the opposite of use, called commonly "from-use," or "ab-use." And it depends on the person, much more than on the article, whether its usefulness or ab-usefulness will be the quality developed in it. Thus, wine, which the Greeks, in their Bacchus, made rightly the type of all passion, and which, when used, "cheereth god and man"[16] (that is to say, strengthens both the divine life, or reasoning power, and the earthy, or carnal power, of man); yet, when abused, becomes "Dionusos," hurtful especially to the divine part of man, or reason.[17] And again, the body itself, being equally liable to use and to abuse, and, when rightly disciplined, serviceable to the State, both for war and labour,—but when not disciplined, or abused, valueless to the State, and capable only of continuing the private or single existence of the individual (and that but feebly)—the Greeks called such a body an "idiotic" or "private" body, from their word signifying a person employed in no way directly useful to the

15. "That which constitutes its (the State's) chief strength" or literally "that in which it may be the most powerful." The passage in Livy from which Ruskin takes this quotation concerns Marcus Curtius who, in obedience to an oracle which demanded that the chief strength of the Roman people be sacrificed, leaped armed and on horseback into a chasm which had appeared in the Roman Forum. In the opinion of Curtius, arms and valor were the chief strength of the Roman people.

16. Judg. 9:13.

17. The actual meaning of the word Dionysus has not been definitely established. It is generally thought the the word is derived from $\Delta\iota\acute{o} + \nu\tilde{\upsilon}\sigma\sigma\varsigma$ or "son of Zeus"; but obviously this derivation makes little sense in the context above. Since Ruskin does not adhere to the conventional spelling of Dionysus and sets the word off in quotation marks, it may be that he is trying to suggest another, and more metaphorical, meaning, namely $\Delta\iota\acute{o} + \nu o\tilde{\upsilon}\sigma o\varsigma$ or "madness or plague of Zeus."

State; whence finally, our "idiot," meaning a person entirely occupied with his own concerns.

Hence, it follows that if a thing is to be useful, it must be not only of an availing nature, but in availing hands. Or, in accurate terms, usefulness is value in the hands of the valiant; so that this science of wealth being, as we have just seen, when regarded as the science of Accumulation, accumulative of capacity as well as of material,—when regarded as the Science of Distribution, is distribution not absolute, but discriminate; not of every thing to every man, but of the right thing to the right man. A difficult science, dependent on more than arithmetic.

64. Wealth, therefore, is "THE POSSESSION OF THE VALUABLE BY THE VALIANT";[18] and in considering it as a power existing in a nation, the two elements, the value of the thing, and the valour of its possessor, must be estimated together. Whence it appears that many of the persons commonly considered wealthy, are in reality no more wealthy than the locks of their own strong boxes are, they being inherently and eternally incapable of wealth; and operating for the nation, in an economical point of view, either as pools of dead water, and eddies in a stream (which, so long as the stream flows, are useless, or serve only to drown people, but may become of importance in a state of stagnation should the stream dry); or else, as dams in a river, of which the ultimate service depends not on the dam, but the miller; or else, as mere accidental stays and impediments, acting not as wealth, but (for we ought to have a correspondent term) as "illth," causing various devastation and trouble around them in all directions; or lastly,

18. Cf. with Xenephon's implied definition of wealth in *Economist* i. 10–12 which Ruskin translates as follows in Appendix III to *Munera Pulveris*: "This being so, it follows that things are only property to the man who knows how to use them; as flutes, for instance, are property to the man who can pipe upon them respectably; but to one who knows not how to pipe, they are no property, unless he can get rid of them advantageously. . . . For if they are not sold, the flutes are no property (being serviceable for nothing); but, sold, they become property. To which Socrates made answer,—'and only then if he knows how to sell them, for if he sell them to another man who cannot play on them, still they are no property.' "

act not at all, but are merely animated conditions of delay, (no use being possible of anything they have until they are dead,) in which last condition they are nevertheless often useful *as* delays, and "impedimenta," if a nation is apt to move too fast.

65. This being so, the difficulty of the true science of Political Economy lies not merely in the need of developing manly character to deal with material value, but in the fact, that while the manly character and material value only form wealth by their conjunction, they have nevertheless a mutually destructive operation on each other. For the manly character is apt to ignore, or even cast away, the material value:—whence that of Pope:—

> "Sure, of qualities demanding praise,
>   More go to ruin fortunes, than to raise."[19]

And on the other hand, the material value is apt to undermine the manly character; so that it must be our work, in the issue, to examine what evidence there is of the effect of wealth on the minds of its possessors; also, what kind of person it is who usually sets himself to obtain wealth, and succeeds in doing so; and whether the world owes more gratitude to rich or to poor men, either for their moral influence upon it, or for chief goods, discoveries, and practical advancements. I may, however, anticipate future conclusions, so far as to state that in a community regulated only by laws of demand and supply, but protected from open violence, the persons who become rich are, generally speaking, industrious, resolute, proud, covetous, prompt, methodical, sensible, unimaginative, insensitive, and ignorant. The persons who remain poor are the entirely foolish, the entirely wise,[20] the idle, the reckless, the humble, the thoughtful, the dull, the

---

19. *Moral Essays,* III. 201–202. Ruskin misquotes the first line which should read: "Yet sure, of qualities deserving praise."

20. (Ruskin's note) "ὁ Ζεὺς δήπου πένεται—Arist. *Plut.* 582. It would but weaken the grand words to lean on the preceding ones:—"ὅτι τοῦ Πλούτου παρέχω βελτίονας ἄνδρας, καὶ τὴν γνώμην, καὶ τήν ἰδέαν." [The first of these quotations from Aristophanes' *Plutus* may be translated: "And Zeus who is indeed poor"; the second, "I have furnished better men than Wealth has furnished." The second quotation is from 11. 558–559.]

imaginative, the sensitive, the well-informed, the improvident, the irregularly and impulsively wicked, the clumsy knave, the open thief, and the entirely merciful, just, and godly person.

66. Thus far, then, of wealth. Next, we have to ascertain the nature of PRICE; that is to say, of exchange value, and its expression by currencies.

Note first, of exchange, there can be no *profit* in it. It is only in labour there can be profit—that is to say, a "making in advance," or "making in favour of" (from proficio). In exchange, there is only advantage, *i.e.*, a bringing of vantage or power to the exchanging persons. Thus, one man, by sowing and reaping, turns one measure of corn into two measures. That is Profit. Another, by digging and forging, turns one spade into two spades. That is Profit. But the man who has two measures of corn wants sometimes to dig; and the man who has two spades wants sometimes to eat:—They exchange the gained grain for the gained tool; and both are the better for the exchange; but though there is much advantage in the transaction, there is no profit. Nothing is constructed or produced. Only that which had been before constructed is given to the person by whom it can be used. If labour is necessary to effect the exchange, that labour is in reality involved in the production, and, like all other labour, bears profit. Whatever number of men are concerned in the manufacture, or in the conveyance, have share in the profit; but neither the manufacture nor the conveyance are the exchange, and in the exchange itself there is no profit.

There may, however, be acquisition, which is a very different thing. If, in the exchange, one man is able to give what cost him little labour for what has cost the other much, he "acquires" a certain quantity of the produce of the other's labour. And precisely what he acquires, the other loses. In mercantile language, the person who thus acquires is commonly said to have "made a profit"; and I believe that many of our merchants are seriously under the impression that it is possible for everybody, somehow, to make a profit in this manner. Whereas, by the unfortunate constitution of the world we live in, the laws both of matter and motion have quite rigorously forbidden universal acquisition of this kind. Profit, or material gain, is attainable only by construction or by discovery; not by exchange. Whenever material gain follows exchange, for every *plus* there is a precisely equal *minus*.

Unhappily for the progress of the science of Political Economy, the plus quantities, or—if I may be allowed to coin an awkward plural—the pluses, make a very positive and venerable appearance in the world, so that every one is eager to learn the science which produces results so magnificent; whereas the minuses have, on the other hand, a tendency to retire into back streets, and other places of shade,—or even to get themselves wholly and finally put out of sight in graves: which renders the algebra of this science peculiar, and difficultly legible; a large number of its negative signs being written by the account-keeper in a kind of red ink, which starvation thins, and makes strangely pale, or even quite invisible ink, for the present.

67. The Science of Exchange, or, as I hear it has been proposed to call it, of "Catallactics," considered as one of gain, is, therefore, simply nugatory; but considered as one of acquisition, it is a very curious science, differing in its data and basis from every other science known. Thus:—If I can exchange a needle with a savage for a diamond, my power of doing so depends either on the savage's ignorance of social arrangements in Europe, or on his want of power to take advantage of them, by selling the diamond to any one else for more needles. If, farther, I make the bargain as completely advantageous to myself as possible, by giving to the savage a needle with no eye in it (reaching, thus a sufficiently satisfactory type of the perfect operation of catallactic science), the advantage to me in the entire transaction depends wholly upon the ignorance, powerlessness, or heedlessness of the person dealt with. Do away with these, and catallactic advantage becomes impossible. So far, therefore, as the science of exchange relates to the advantage of one of the exchanging persons only, it is founded on the ignorance or incapacity of the opposite person. Where these vanish, it also vanishes. It is therefore a science founded on nescience, and an art founded on artlessness. But all

other sciences and arts, except this, have for their object the doing away with their opposite nescience and artlessness. *This* science, alone of sciences, must, by all available means, promulgate and prolong its opposite nescience; otherwise the science itself is impossible. It is, therefore, peculiarly and alone the science of darkness; probably a bastard science—not by any means a *divina scientia*, but one begotten of another father, that father who, advising his children to turn stones into bread, is himself employed in turning bread into stones, and who, if you ask a fish of him (fish not being producible on his estate), can but give you a serpent.[21]

68. The general law, then, respecting just or economical exchange, is simply this:—There must be advantage on both sides (or if only advantage on one, at least no disadvantage on the other) to the persons exchanging; and just payment for his time, intelligence, and labour, to any intermediate person effecting the transaction (commonly called a merchant); and whatever advantage there is on either side, and whatever pay is given to the intermediate persons, should be thoroughly known to all concerned. All attempt at concealment implies some practice of the opposite, or undivine science, founded on nescience. Whence another saving of the Jew merchant's—"As a nail between the stone joints, so doth sin stick fast between buying and selling."[22] Which peculiar riveting of stone and timber, in men's dealings with each other, is again set forth in the house which was to be destroyed—timber and stones together—when Zechariah's roll (more probably "curved sword")[23] flew over it: "the curse that goeth forth over all the earth upon every one that stealeth and holdeth himself guiltless,"[24] instantly followed by the vision of the Great Measure;—the measure "of the injustice of them in all of earth" (αὕτη ἡ ἀδικία αὐτῶν ἐν πάσῃ τῇ γῇ), with the weight

21. Matt. 8:10.
22. Eccles. 27:2.
23. Zech. 5:2. In this and the next two notes, Ruskin is quoting from the Septuagint Version of the Bible.
24. Zech. 5:3 ff.

of lead for its lid, and the woman, the spirit of wickedness, within it;—that is to say, Wickedness hidden by dulness, and formalized, outwardly, into ponderously established cruelty. "It shall be set upon its own base in the land of Babel."[25]

69. I have hitherto carefully restricted myself, in speaking of exchange, to the use of the term "advantage"; but that term includes two ideas: the advantage, namely, of getting what we *need*, and that of getting what we *wish for*. Three-fourths of the demands existing in the world are romantic; founded on visions, idealisms, hopes, and affections; and the regulation of the purse is, in its essence, regulation of the imagination and the heart. Hence, the right discussion of the nature of price is a very high metaphysical and psychical problem; sometimes to be solved only in a passionate manner, as by David in his counting the price of the water of the well by the gate of Bethlehem;[26] but its first conditions are the following:—The price of anything is the quantity of labour given by the person desiring it, in order to obtain possession of it. This price depends on four variable quantities. *A*. The quantity of wish the purchaser has for the thing; opposed to α, the quantity of wish the seller has to keep it. *B*. The quantity of labour the purchaser can afford, to obtain the thing; opposed to β, the quantity of labour the seller can afford, to keep it. These quantities are operative only in excess: *i.e.*, the quantity of wish (*A*) means the quantity of wish for this thing, above wish for other things; and the quantity of work (*B*) means the quantity which can be spared to get this thing from the quantity needed to get other things.

Phenomena of price, therefore, are intensely complex, curious, and interesting—too complex, however, to be examined yet; every one of them, when traced far enough, showing itself at last as a part of the bargain of the Poor of the Flock (or "flock of slaughter"[27]), "If ye think good, give ME my price, and if not, forbear"—

25. (Ruskin's note) Zech. v. 11. See note on the passage, at p. 148. [Here p. 84.]
26. II Sam. 23:15–16.
27. Zech. 11:7.

Zech. xi. 12; but as the price of everything is to be calculated finally in labour, it is necessary to define the nature of that standard.

70. Labour is the contest of the life of man with an opposite; —the term "life" including his intellect, soul, and physical power, contending with question, difficulty, trial, or material force.

Labour is of a higher or lower order, as it includes more or fewer of the elements of life: and labour of good quality, in any kind, includes always as much intellect and feeling as will fully and harmoniously regulate the physical force.

In speaking of the value and price of labour, it is necessary always to understand labour of a given rank and quality, as we should speak of gold or silver of a given standard. Bad (that is, heartless, inexperienced, or senseless) labour cannot be valued; it is like gold of uncertain alloy, or flawed iron.[28]

The quality and kind of labour being given, its value, like that of all other valuable things, is invariable. But the quantity of it which must be given for other things is variable: and in estimating this variation, the price of other things must always be counted by the quantity of labour; not the price of labour by the quantity of other things.

71. Thus, if we want to plant an apple sapling in rocky ground, it may take two hours' work; in soft ground, perhaps only half an hour. Grant the soil equally good for the tree in

---

28. (Ruskin's note) Labour which is entirely good of its kind, that is to say, effective, or efficient, the Greeks called "weighable," or ἄξιος, translated usually "worthy," and because thus substantial and true, they called its price τιμή, the "honourable estimate" of it (honorarium): this word being founded on their conception of true labour as a divine thing, to be honoured with the kind of honour given to the gods; whereas the price of false labour, or of that which led away from life, was to be, not honour, but vengeance; for which they reserved another word, attributing the exaction of such price to a peculiar goddess, called Tisiphone, the "requiter (or quittance-taker) of death"; a person versed in the highest branches of arithmetic, and punctual in her habits; with whom accounts current have been opened also in modern days. [The Greek word for vengeance to which Ruskin alludes is τίσις. Tisiphone is one of the Eumenides; her name means "blood-avenger."]

each case. Then the value of the sapling planted by two hours' work is nowise greater than that of the sapling planted in half an hour. One will bear no more fruit than the other. Also, one half-hour of work is as valuable as another half-hour; nevertheless, the one sapling has cost four such pieces of work, the other only one. Now, the proper statement of this fact is, not that the labour on the hard ground is cheaper than on the soft; but that the tree is dearer. The exchange value may, or may not, afterwards depend on this fact. If other people have plenty of soft ground to plant in, they will take no cognizance of our two hours' labour in the price they will offer for the plant on the rock. And if, through want of sufficient botanical science, we have planted an upas-tree[29] instead of an apple, the exchange value will be a negative quantity; still less proportionate to the labour expended.

What is commonly called cheapness of labour, signifies, therefore, in reality, that many obstacles have to be overcome by it; so that much labour is required to produce a small result. But this should never be spoken of as cheapness of labour, but as dearness of the object wrought for. It would be just as rational to say that walking was cheap, because we had ten miles to walk home to our dinner, as that labour was cheap, because we had to work ten hours to earn it.

72. The last word which we have to define is "Production."

I have hitherto spoken of all labour as profitable; because it is impossible to consider under one head the quality or value of labour, and its aim. But labour of the best quality may be various in aim. It may be either constructive ("gathering," from con and struo), as agriculture; nugatory, as jewel-cutting; or destructive ("scattering," from de and struo), as war. It is not, however, always easy to prove labour, apparently nugatory, to be actually so;[30] generally, the formula holds good: "he that gathereth not,

29. A fabulous tree alleged to have existed in Java. Its properties were believed to be so poisonous as to destroy all animal and vegetable life for a considerable distance around it.

30. (Ruskin's note) The most accurately nugatory labour is, perhaps, that

scattereth";[31] thus, the jeweller's art is probably very harmful in
its ministering to a clumsy and inelegant pride. So that, finally, I
believe nearly all labour may be shortly divided into positive
and negative labour: positive, that which produces life; negative,
that which produces death; the most directly negative labour
being murder, and the most directly positive, the bearing and
rearing of children: so that in the precise degree in which murder
is hateful, on the negative side of idleness, in that exact degree
child-rearing is admirable, on the positive side of idleness. For
which reason, and because of the honour that there is in rearing[32]
children, while the wife is said to be as the vine (for cheering),
the children are as the olive branch,[33] for praise: nor for praise
only, but for peace (because large families can only be reared in
times of peace): though since, in their spreading and voyaging in

---

of which not enough is given to answer a purpose effectually, and which,
therefore, has all to be done over again. Also, labour which fails of effect
through non-co-operation. The curé of a little village near Bellinzona, to
whom I had expressed wonder that the peasants allowed the Ticino to flood
their fields, told me that they would not join to build an effectual embankment high up the valley, because everybody said "that would help his neighbours as much as himself." So every proprietor built a bit of low embankment
about his own field; and the Ticino, as soon as it had a mind, swept away
and swallowed all up together.

31. Matt. 12:30.

32. (Ruskin's note) Observe, I say, "rearing," not "begetting." The praise
is in the seventh season, not in σπορητός, nor in φυταλία, but in ὀπώρα. It
is strange that men always praise enthusiastically any person who, by a momentary exertion, saves a life; but praise very hesitatingly a person who, by
exertion and self-denial prolonged through years, creates one. We give the
crown "ob civem servatum";—why not "ob civem natum"? Born, I mean, to
the full, in soul as well as body. England has oak enough, I think, for both
chaplets. [Ruskin's reference to the seven seasons is based on Galen's discussion of them in On the Natural Faculties vi. 127 except that he changes their
order: ἔαρ (the spring), θέρος (the summer), ὀπώρα (the dog-days, the season
of ripe fruit), φθινόπωρον (the autumn), σπορητός (the seed time), χειμών
(the winter), φυταλία (the planting time). The two Latin phrases in the note
may be translated respectively "as recompense for saving a citizen" and "as
recompense for producing a citizen."]

33. Ps. 128:3.

various directions, they distribute strength, they are, to the home strength, as arrows in the hand of the giant[34]—striking here and there far away.

Labour being thus various in its result, the prosperity of any nation is in exact proportion to the quantity of labour which it spends in obtaining and employing means of life. Observe,—I say, obtaining and employing; that is to say, not merely wisely producing, but wisely distributing and consuming. Economists usually speak as if there were no good in consumption absolute.[35] So far from this being so, consumption absolute is the end, crown, and perfection of production; and wise consumption is a far more difficult art than wise production. Twenty people can gain money for one who can use it; and the vital question, for individual and for nation, is, never "how much do they make?" but "to what purpose do they spend?"

73. The reader may, perhaps, have been surprised at the slight reference I have hitherto made to "capital," and its functions. It is here the place to define them.

Capital signifies "head, or source, or root material"—it is material by which some derivative or secondary good is produced. It is only capital proper (caput vivum, not caput mortuum)[36] when it is thus producing something different from itself. It is a root, which does not enter into vital function till it produces something else than a root: namely, fruit. That fruit will in time again produce roots; and so all living capital issues in reproduction of capital; but capital which produces nothing but capital is only root producing root; bulb issuing in bulb, never in tulip; seed issuing in seed, never in bread. The Political Economy of Europe has hitherto devoted itself wholly to the multiplication,

34. Ps. 127:4.

35. (Ruskin's note) When Mr. Mill speaks of productive consumption, he only means consumption which results in increase of capital or material wealth. See I. iii. 4, and I. iii. 5.

36. Literally, "a living head, not a dead head." Alchemists used the term "caput mortuum" to designate the residuum after the distillation or sublimation of any substance.

or (less even) the aggregation, of bulbs. It never saw, nor conceived, such a thing as a tulip. Nay, boiled bulbs they might have
been—glass bulbs—Prince Rupert's drops,[37] consummated in pow-
der (well, if it were glass-powder and not gunpowder), for any
end or meaning the economists had in defining the laws of aggregation. We will try and get a clearer notion of them.

The best and simplest general type of capital is a well-made
ploughshare. Now, if that ploughshare did nothing but beget
other ploughshares, in a polypous manner,—however the great
cluster of polypous plough might glitter in the sun, it would
have lost its function of capital. It becomes true capital only
by another kind of splendour,—when it is seen "splendescere
sulco,"[38] to grow bright in the furrow; rather with diminution
of its substance, than addition, by the noble friction. And the
true home question, to every capitalist and to every nation, is
not, "how many ploughs have you?" but, "where are your fur-
rows?" not—"how quickly will this capital reproduce itself?"—but,
"what will it do during reproduction?" What substance will it
furnish, good for life? what work construct, protective of life? if
none, its own reproduction is useless—if worse than none,—(for
capital may destroy life as well as support it), its own reproduction is worse than useless; it is merely an advance from Tisiphone,[39] on mortgage—not a profit by any means.

74. Not a profit, as the ancients truly saw, and showed in the
type of Ixion;[40]—for capital is the head, or fountain head, of

37. Pear-shaped pieces of glass, made by dropping molten glass into water.
The drops burst into fragments if the slender tail is broken. They were introduced into England from Germany by the nephew of Charles I, Prince Rupert
(1619–82).

38. Virgil *Georgics* i. 46.

39. For an earlier reference to Tisiphone, see note 28 above.

40. Ixion, a king of Thessaly, married Dis, the daughter of Deioneus, and
then refused to pay the bridal gifts that he had promised. Deioneus then
resorted to violence and stole some of Ixion's horses. Concealing his resentment, Ixion invited Deioneus to a banquet and when he arrived threw him
into a pit of burning coals. When no one would purify him of this treach-
erous murder, Zeus took pity on him and carried him up to heaven. But

wealth—the "well-head" of wealth, as the clouds are the well-
heads of rain: but when clouds are without water,[41] and only
beget clouds, they issue in wrath at last, instead of rain, and in
lightning instead of harvest; whence Ixion is said first to have
invited his guests to a banquet, and then made them fall into a
pit filled with fire; which is the type of the temptation of riches
issuing in imprisoned torment,—torment in a pit, (as also Demas'
silver mine,[42]) after which, to show the rage of riches passing from
lust of pleasure to lust of power, yet power not truly understood,
Ixion is said to have desired Juno, and instead, embracing a
cloud (or phantasm), to have begotten the Centaurs; the power
of mere wealth being, in itself, as the embrace of a shadow,—com-
fortless, (so also "Ephraim feedeth on wind and followeth after
the east wind";[43] or "that which is not"—Prov. xxiii. 5; and again
Dante's Geryon,[44] the type of avaricious fraud, as he flies, gathers
the *air* up with retractile claws,—"l'aer a se raccolse,"[45]) but in its

instead of showing his gratitude, Ixion attempted to win the love of Hera
and boasted that he had done so. Zeus, angered by his insolence, created a
phantom resembling Hera, and by it Ixion became the father of a Centaur.
For his gross ingratitude, Ixion was severely punished in Hades; his hands
and feet were chained to a wheel which rolled perpetually in the air.

Ruskin's interpretation of the legend of Ixion appears to be based on the
legend as it is presented by Pindar in *Pythia* 2. 34–88, for Pindar uses the
legend to illustrate the moral "Requite their love from whom your blessings
rise" and later in the ode he maintains that wealth is worthless if it is not
accompanied by wisdom.

41. Jude 12.

42. An allusion to Bunyan's *Pilgrim's Progress*, Part I. Demas' silver mine
(named after one of Paul's disciples who abandoned him in his last days
because "his heart was set on this world") located in the Hill called Lucre
attracted travelers "because of the rarity of it." Those who went too near
the edge of the pit fell in and were either slain, maimed, or "could not to
their dying day be their own men again."

43. Hos. 12:1.

44. *Inferno*, XVII.

45. (Ruskin's note) So also in the vision of the women bearing the ephah,
before quoted, "the wind was in their wings," not wings "of a stork," as in
our version; but "*milvi*," of a kite, in the Vulgate, or perhaps more accurately
still in the Septuagint, "hoopoe," a bird connected typically with the power

offspring, a mingling of the brutal with the human nature: human in sagacity—using both intellect and arrow; but brutal in its body and hoof, for consuming, and trampling down. For which sin Ixion is at last bound upon a wheel—fiery and toothed, and rolling perpetually in the air;—the type of human labour when selfish and fruitless (kept far into the Middle Ages in their wheel of fortune); the wheel which has in it no breath or spirit, but is whirled by chance only; whereas of all true work the Ezekiel vision is true, that the Spirit of the living creature is in the wheels, and where the angels go, the wheels go by them;[46] but move no otherwise.

75. This being the real nature of capital, it follows that there are two kinds of true production, always going on in an active State: one of seed, and one of food; or production for the Ground, and for the Mouth; both of which are by covetous persons thought to be production only for the granary; whereas the function of the granary is but intermediate and conservative, fulfilled in distribution; else it ends in nothing but mildew, and nourishment of rats and worms. And since production for the Ground is only useful with future hope of harvest, all *essential* production is for the Mouth; and is finally measured by the mouth; hence, as I said above, consumption is the crown of production; and the wealth of a nation is only to be estimated by what it consumes.

The want of any clear sight of this fact is the capital error,

---

of riches by many traditions, of which that of its petition for a crest of gold is perhaps the most interesting. The "Birds" of Aristophanes, in which its part is principal, are full of them; note especially the "fortification of the air with baked bricks, like Babylon," L. 550; and, again, compare the Plutus of Dante, who (to show the influence of riches in destroying the reason) is the only one of the powers of the Inferno who cannot speak intelligibly; and also the cowardliest; he is not merely quelled or restrained, but literally "collapses" at a word; the sudden and helpless operation of mercantile panic being all told in the brief metaphor, "as the sails, swollen with the wind, fall, when the mast breaks." [The vision of "the women bearing the ephah" appears in Zech. 5:3–9 and is "quoted" in paragraph 68 above. For the source of the quotation at the end of the note, see *Inferno*, VII.]

46. Ezek. 1:15 ff.

issuing in rich interest and revenue of error among the political
economists. Their minds are continually set on money-gain, not
on mouth-gain; and they fall into every sort of net and snare,
dazzled by the coin-glitter as birds by the fowler's glass; or rather
(for there is not much else like birds in them) they are like children trying to jump on the heads of their own shadows; the
money-gain being only the shadow of the true gain, which is
humanity.

76. The final object of political economy, therefore, is to get
good method of consumption, and great quantity of consumption: in other words, to use everything, and to use it nobly;
whether it be substance, service, or service perfecting substance.
The most curious error in Mr. Mill's entire work, (provided for
him originally by Ricardo,) is his endeavour to distinguish between direct and indirect service, and consequent assertion that
a demand for commodities is not demand for labour (I. v. 9, *et
seq.*). He distinguishes between labourers employed to lay out
pleasure grounds, and to manufacture velvet; declaring that it
makes material difference to the labouring classes in which of
these two ways a capitalist spends his money; because the employment of the gardeners is a demand for labour, but the purchase
of velvet is not.[47] Error colossal, as well as strange. It will, indeed,

47. (Ruskin's note) The value of raw material, which has, indeed, to be
deducted from the price of the labour, is not contemplated in the passages
referred to, Mr. Mill having fallen into the mistake solely by pursuing the
collateral results of the payment of wages to middlemen. He says—"The consumer does not, with his own funds, pay the weaver for his day's work."
Pardon me: the consumer of the velvet pays the weaver with his own funds
as much as he pays the gardener. He pays, probably, an intermediate ship-
owner, velvet merchant, and shopman; pays carriage money, shop rent, damage
money, time money, and care money; all these are above and beside the
velvet price, (just as the wages of a head gardener would be above the grass
price); but the velvet is as much produced by the consumer's capital, though
he does not pay for it till six months after production, as the grass is produced by his capital, though he does not pay the man who rolled and mowed
it on Monday, till Saturday afternoon. I do not know if Mr. Mill's conclusion,—"the capital cannot be dispensed with, the purchasers can" (p. 98), has
yet been reduced to practice in the City on any large scale.

make a difference to the labourer whether we bid him swing his
scythe in the spring winds, or drive the loom in pestilential air;
but, so far as his pocket is concerned, it makes to him absolutely
no difference whether we order him to make green velvet, with
seed and a scythe, or red velvet, with silk and scissors. Neither
does it anywise concern him whether, when the velvet is made,
we consume it by walking on it, or wearing it, so long as our
consumption of it is wholly selfish. But if our consumption is to
be in anywise unselfish, not only our mode of consuming the
articles we require interests him, but also the *kind* of article we
require with a view to consumption. As thus (returning for a
moment to Mr. Mill's great hardware theory[48]): it matters, so far
as the labourer's immediate profit is concerned, not an iron filing
whether I employ him in growing a peach, or forging a bomb-
shell; but my probable mode of consumption of those articles
matters seriously. Admit that it is to be in both cases "unselfish,"
and the difference, to him, is final, whether when his child is ill,
I walk into his cottage and give it the peach, or drop the shell
down his chimney, and blow his roof off.

The worst of it, for the peasant, is, that the capitalist's consumption of the peach is apt to be selfish, and of the shell, dis-
tributive;[49] but, in all cases, this is the broad and general fact,

48. (Ruskin's note) Which, observe, is the precise opposite of the one under
examination. The hardware theory required us to discharge our gardeners
and engage manufacturers; the velvet theory requires us to discharge our
manufacturers and engage gardeners.

49. (Ruskin's note) It is one very awful form of the operation of wealth
in Europe that it is entirely capitalists' wealth which supports unjust wars.
Just wars do not need so much money to support them; for most of the men
who wage such, wage them gratis; but for an unjust war, men's bodies and
souls have both to be bought; and the best tools of war for them besides;
which makes such war costly to the maximum; not to speak of the cost of base
fear, and angry suspicion, between nations which have not grace nor honesty
enough in all their multitudes to buy an hour's peace of mind with: as, at
present, France and England, purchasing of each other ten millions sterling
worth of consternation annually, (a remarkably light crop, half thorns and
half aspen leaves,—sown, reaped, and granaried by the "science" of the modern political economist, teaching covetousness instead of truth). And all unjust

that on due catallactic commercial principles, *somebody's* roof must go off in fulfilment of the bomb's destiny. You may grow for your neighbour, at your liking, grapes or grape-shot; he will also, catallactically, grow grapes or grape-shot for you, and you will each reap what you have sown.[50]

77. It is, therefore, the manner and issue of consumption which are the real tests of production. Production does not consist in things laboriously made, but in things serviceably consumable; and the question for the nation is not how much labour it employs, but how much life it produces. For as consumption is the end and aim of production, so life is the end and aim of consumption.

I left this question to the reader's thought two months ago,[51] choosing rather that he should work it out for himself than have it sharply stated to him. But now, the ground being sufficiently broken (and the details into which the several questions, here opened, must lead us, being too complex for discussion in the pages of a periodical, so that I must pursue them elsewhere), I desire, in closing the series of introductory papers, to leave this one great fact clearly stated. There is no Wealth but Life. Life, including all its powers of love, of joy, and of admiration.[52] That country is the richest which nourishes the greatest number of noble and happy human beings; that man is richest who, having perfected the functions of his own life to the utmost, has also the widest helpful influence, both personal, and by means of his possessions, over the lives of others.

A strange political economy; the only one, nevertheless, that

war being supportable, if not by pillage of the enemy, only by loans from capitalists, these loans are repaid by subsequent taxation of the people, who appear to have no will in the matter, the capitalists' will being the primary root of the war; but its real root is the covetousness of the whole nation, rendering it incapable of faith, frankness, or justice, and bringing about, therefore, in due time, his own separate loss and punishment to each person.

50. Gal. 6:7.

51. See paragraphs 40–41 above.

52. Cf. with Wordsworth's *The Excursion*, iv. 763: "We live by Admiration, Hope and Love."

ever was or can be: all political economy founded on self-interest[53] being but the fulfilment of that which once brought schism into the Policy of angels, and ruin into the Economy of Heaven.[54]

78. "The greatest number of human beings noble and happy." But is the nobleness consistent with the number? Yes, not only consistent with it, but essential to it. The maximum of life can only be reached by the maximum of virtue. In this respect the law of human population differs wholly from that of animal life. The multiplication of animals is checked only by want of food, and by the hostility of races; the population of the gnat is restrained by the hunger of the swallow, and that of the swallow by the scarcity of gnats. Man, considered as an animal, is indeed limited by the same laws: hunger, or plague, or war, are the necessary and only restraints upon his increase,—effectual restraints hitherto,—his principal study having been how most swiftly to destroy himself, or ravage his dwelling-places, and his highest skill directed to give range to the famine, seed to the plague, and sway to the sword. But, considered as other than an animal, his increase is not limited by these laws. It is limited only by the limits of his courage and his love. Both of these *have* their bounds; and ought to have; his race has its bounds also; but these have not yet been reached, nor will be reached for ages.

79. In all the ranges of human thought I know none so melancholy as the speculations of political economists on the population question. It is proposed to better the condition of the labourer by giving him higher wages. "Nay," says the economist, —"if you raise his wages, he will either people down to the same point of misery at which you found him, or drink your wages away." He will. I know it. Who gave him this will? Suppose it were your own son of whom you spoke, declaring to me that you dared not take him into your firm, nor even give him

53. (Ruskin's note) "In all reasoning about prices, the proviso must be understood, 'supposing all parties to take care of their own interest.' "—Mill, III. i. 5.

54. II Pet. 2:3–4.

his just labourer's wages, because if you did he would die of drunkenness, and leave half a score of children to the parish. "Who gave your son these dispositions?"—I should enquire. Has he them by inheritance or by education? By one or other they *must* come; and as in him, so also in the poor. Either these poor are of a race essentially different from ours, and unredeemable (which, however often implied, I have heard none yet openly say), or else by such care as we have ourselves received, we may make them continent and sober as ourselves—wise and dispassionate as we are—models arduous of imitation. "But," it is answered, "they cannot receive education." Why not? That is precisely the point at issue. Charitable persons suppose the worst fault of the rich is to refuse the people meat; and the people cry for their meat, kept back by fraud, to the Lord of Multitudes.[55] Alas! it

55. (Ruskin's note) James v. 4. Observe, in these statements I am not taking up, nor countenancing one whit, the common socialist idea of division of property: division of property is its destruction; and with it the destruction of all hope, all industry, and all justice: it is simply chaos—a chaos towards which the believers in modern political economy are fast tending, and from which I am striving to save them. The rich man does not keep back meat from the poor by retaining his riches; but by basely using them. Riches are a form of strength; and a strong man does not injure others by keeping his strength, but by using it injuriously. The socialist, seeing a strong man oppress a weak one, cries out—"Break the strong man's arms;" but I say, "Teach him to use them to better purpose." The fortitude and intelligence which acquire riches are intended, by the Giver of both, not to scatter, nor to give away, but to employ those riches in the service of mankind; in other words, in the redemption of the erring and aid of the weak—that is to say, there is first to be the work to gain money; then the Sabbath of use for it—the Sabbath, whose law is, not to lose life, but to save. It is continually the fault or the folly of the poor that they are poor, as it is usually a child's fault if it falls into a pond, and a cripple's weakness that slips at a crossing; nevertheless, most passers-by would pull the child out, or help up the cripple. Put it at the worst, that all the poor of the world are but disobedient children, or careless cripples, and that all rich people are wise and strong, and you will see at once that neither is the socialist right in desiring to make everybody poor, powerless, and foolish as he is himself, nor the rich man right in leaving the children in the mire. [For the source of the Biblical allusion in the note, see Luke 13:14 ff.]

is not meat of which the refusal is cruelest, or to which the claim is validest. The life is more than the meat.[56] The rich not only refuse food to the poor; they refuse wisdom; they refuse virtue; they refuse salvation. Ye sheep without shepherd,[57] it is not the pasture that has been shut from you, but the Presence. Meat! perhaps your right to that may be pleadable; but other rights have to be pleaded first. Claim your crumbs from the table if you will; but claim them as children, not as dogs; claim your right to be fed, but claim more loudly your right to be holy, perfect, and pure.

Strange words to be used of working people! "What! holy; without any long robes or anointing oils; these rough-jacketed, rough-worded persons; set to nameless, dishonoured service? Perfect!—these, with dim eyes and cramped limbs, and slowly wakening minds? Pure!—these, with sensual desire and grovelling thought; foul of body and coarse of soul?" It may be so; nevertheless, such as they are, they are the holiest, perfectest, purest persons the earth can at present show. They may be what you have said; but if so, they yet are holier than we who have left them thus.

But what can be done for them? Who can clothe—who teach—who restrain their multitudes? What end can there be for them at last, but to consume one another?

I hope for another end, though not, indeed, from any of the three remedies for over-population commonly suggested by economists.

80. These three are, in brief—Colonization; Bringing in of waste lands; or Discouragement of Marriage.

The first and second of these expedients merely evade or delay the question. It will, indeed, be long before the world has been all colonized, and its deserts all brought under cultivation. But the radical question is, not how much habitable land is in the world,

56. Matt. 6:25.
57. Num. 27:17; Matt. 9:36.

but how many human beings ought to be maintained on a given space of habitable land.

Observe, I say, *ought* to be, not how many *can* be. Ricardo, with his usual inaccuracy, defines what he calls the "natural rate of wages" as "that which will maintain the labourer."[58] Maintain him! yes; but how?—the question was instantly thus asked of me by a working girl, to whom I read the passage. I will amplify her question for her. "Maintain him, how?" As, first, to what length of life? Out of a given number of fed persons, how many are to be old—how many young? that is to say, will you arrange their maintenance so as to kill them early—say at thirty or thirty-five on the average, including deaths of weakly or ill-fed children?— or so as to enable them to live out a natural life? You will feed a greater number, in the first case,[59] by rapidity of succession; probably a happier number in the second: which does Mr. Ricardo mean to be their natural state, and to which state belongs the natural rate of wages?

Again: A piece of land which will only support ten idle, ignorant, and improvident persons, will support thirty or forty intelligent and industrious ones. Which of these is their natural state, and to which of them belongs the natural rate of wages?

Again: If a piece of land support forty persons in industrious ignorance; and if, tired of this ignorance, they set apart ten of their number to study the properties of cones, and the sizes of stars; the labour of these ten being withdrawn from the ground, must either tend to the increase of food in some transitional manner, or the persons set apart for sidereal and conic purposes must starve, or some one else starve instead of them. What is, therefore, the natural rate of wages of the scientific persons, and how does this rate relate to, or measure, their reverted or transitional productiveness?

Again: If the ground maintains, at first, forty labourers in a peaceable and pious state of mind, but they become in a few

58. *Principles of Political Economy and Taxation*, chap. v.

59. (Ruskin's note) The quantity of life is the same in both cases; but it is differently allotted.

years so quarrelsome and impious that they have to set apart five, to meditate upon and settle their disputes;—ten, armed to the teeth with costly instruments, to enforce the decisions; and five to remind everybody in an eloquent manner of the existence of a God;—what will be the result upon the general power of production, and what is the "natural rate of wages" of the meditative, muscular, and oracular labourers?

81. Leaving these questions to be discussed, or waived, at their pleasure, by Mr. Ricardo's followers, I proceed to state the main facts bearing on that probable future of the labouring classes which has been partially glanced at by Mr. Mill. That chapter and the preceding one[60] differ from the common writing of political economists in admitting some value in the aspect of nature, and expressing regret at the probability of the destruction of natural scenery. But we may spare our anxieties on this head. Men can neither drink steam, nor eat stone. The maximum of population on a given space of land implies also the relative maximum of edible vegetable, whether for men or cattle; it implies a maximum of pure air, and of pure water. Therefore: a maximum of wood, to transmute the air, and of sloping ground, protected by herbage from the extreme heat of the sun, to feed the streams. All England may, if it so chooses, become one manufacturing town; and Englishmen, sacrificing themselves to the good of general humanity, may live diminished lives in the midst of noise, of darkness, and of deadly exhalation. But the world cannot become a factory nor a mine. No amount of ingenuity will ever make iron digestible by the million, nor substitute hydrogen for wine. Neither the avarice nor the rage of men will ever feed them; and however the apple of Sodom and the grape of Gomorrah may spread their table for a time with dainties of ashes, and nectar of asps,—so long as men live by bread, the far away valleys must laugh as they are covered with the gold of God, and the shouts of His happy multitudes ring round the winepress and the well.

60. *Principles of Political Economy*, Bk. IV. chap. vii ("On the Probable Futurity of the Labouring Classes") and chap. vi ("Of the Stationary State").

82. Nor need our more sentimental economists fear the too wide spread of the formalities of a mechanical agriculture. The presence of a wise population implies the search for felicity as well as for food; nor can any population reach its maximum but through that wisdom which "rejoices"[61] in the habitable parts of the earth. The desert has its appointed place and work; the eternal engine, whose beam is the earth's axle, whose beat is its year, and whose breath is its ocean, will still divide imperiously to their desert kingdoms bound with unfurrowable rock, and swept by unarrested sand, their powers of frost and fire: but the zones and lands between, habitable, will be loveliest in habitation. The desire of the heart is also the light of the eyes.[62] No scene is continually and untiringly loved, but one rich by joyful human labour; smooth in field; fair in garden; full in orchard; trim, sweet, and frequent in homestead; ringing with voices of vivid existence. No air is sweet that is silent; it is only sweet when full of low currents of under sound—triplets of birds, and murmur and chirp of insects, and deep-toned words of men, and wayward trebles of childhood. As the art of life is learned, it will be found at last that all lovely things are also necessary;—the wild flower by the wayside, as well as the tended corn; and the wild birds and creatures of the forest, as well as the tended cattle; because man doth not live by bread only,[63] but also by the desert manna; by every wondrous word and unknowable work of God. Happy, in that he knew them not, nor did his fathers know; and that round about him reaches yet into the infinite, the amazement of his existence.

83. Note, finally, that all effectual advancement towards this true felicity of the human race must be by individual, not public effort. Certain general measures may aid, certain revised laws guide, such advancement; but the measure and law which have first to be determined are those of each man's home. We continually hear it recommended by sagacious people to complaining

61. Prov. 8:31.
62. Prov. 15:30.
63. Deut. 8:3; Matt. 4:4; Job 37:14.

neighbours (usually less well placed in the world than themselves), that they should "remain content in the station in which Providence has placed them."[64] There are perhaps some circumstances of life in which Providence has no intention that people *should* be content. Nevertheless, the maxim is on the whole a good one; but it is peculiarly for home use. That your neighbour should, or should not, remain content with *his* position, is not your business; but it is very much your business to remain content with your own. What is chiefly needed in England at the present day is to show the quantity of pleasure that may be obtained by a consistent, well-administered competence, modest, confessed, and laborious. We need examples of people who, leaving Heaven to decide whether they are to rise in the world, decide for themselves that they will be happy in it, and have resolved to seek—not greater wealth, but simpler pleasure; not higher fortune, but deeper felicity; making the first of possessions, self-possession; and honouring themselves in the harmless pride and calm pursuits of peace.

Of which lowly peace it is written that "justice and peace have kissed each other"; and that the fruit of justice is "sown in peace of them that make peace";[65] not "peace-makers" in the common understanding—reconcilers of quarrels; (though that function also follows on the greater one;) but peace-Creators; Givers of Calm. Which you cannot give, unless you first gain; nor is this gain one which will follow assuredly on any course of business, commonly so called. No form of gain is less probable, business being (as is shown in the language of all nations—πωλεῖν from πέλω, πρᾶσις from περάω, venire, vendre, and venal, from venio, etc.[66]) essentially restless—and probably contentious;—hav-

64. A reference to one of the *Answers* in the Anglican Catechism: "And to do my duty in that state of life unto which shall please God to call me."
65. Ps. 85:10; Jas. 3:18.
66. In this parenthetical remark, Ruskin attempts to demonstrate the etymological relationship between words signifying the more simple forms of activity and words denoting economic exchange. The Greek word πωλεῖν, 'to sell," is derived from πέλω, "to be about"; the Latin word *venire*, "to

ing a raven-like mind to the motion to and fro, as to the carrion food; whereas the olive-feeding and bearing birds look for rest for their feet;[67] thus it is said of Wisdom that she "hath builded her house, and hewn out her seven pillars";[68] and even when, though apt to wait long at the doorposts, she has to leave her house and go abroad, her paths are peace[69] also.

84. For us, at all events, her work must begin at the entry of the doors: all true economy is "Law of the house." Strive to make that law strict, simple, generous: waste nothing, and grudge nothing. Care in nowise to make more of money, but care to make much of it; remembering always the great, palpable, inevitable fact—the rule and root of all economy—that what one person has, another cannot have; and that every atom of substance, of whatever kind, used or consumed, is so much human life spent; which, if it issue in the saving present life, or gaining more, is well spent, but if not is either so much life prevented, or so much slain. In all buying, consider, first, what condition of existence you cause in the producers of what you buy; secondly, whether the sum you have paid is just to the producer, and in due proportion, lodged in his hands;[70] thirdly, to how much clear use, for food, knowledge, or joy, this that you have bought can be put; and fourthly, to whom and in what way it can be most

---

sell," the French word *vendre*, "a sale," and the English word *venal*, meaning something "capable of being bought" are all ultimately derived from the Latin verb *venio*, meaning "to come" or "to go." The word πρᾶσις represents an error in the text; in *Cornhill Magazine*, Ruskin gave the word as πρᾶσις, "a sale," which is derived from περάω, meaning "to carry beyond the seas."

67. Gen. 8:7.

68. Prov. 9:1.

69. Prov. 3:17.

70. (Ruskin's note) The proper offices of middlemen, namely, overseers (or authoritative workmen), conveyancers (merchants, sailors, retail dealers, etc.), and order-takers (persons employed to receive directions from the consumer), must, of course, be examined before I can enter farther into the question of just payment of the first producer. But I have not spoken of them in these introductory papers, because the evils attendant on the abuse of such intermediate functions result not from any alleged principle of modern political economy, but from private carelessness or iniquity.

speedily and serviceably distributed; in all dealings whatsoever insisting on entire openness and stern fulfilment; and in all doings, on perfection and loveliness of accomplishment; especially on fineness and purity of all marketable commodity: watching at the same time for all ways of gaining, or teaching, powers of simple pleasure; and of showing "ὅσον ἐν ἀσφδέλῳ μέγ᾽ ὄνειαρ"[71] the sum of enjoyment depending not on the quantity of things tasted, but on the vivacity and patience of taste.

85. And if, on due and honest thought over these things, it seems that the kind of existence to which men are now summoned by every plea of pity and claim of right, may, for some time at least, not be a luxurious one;—consider whether, even supposing it guiltless, luxury would be desired by any of us, if we saw clearly at our sides the suffering which accompanies it in the world. Luxury is indeed possible in the future—innocent and exquisite; luxury for all, and by the help of all; but luxury at present can only be enjoyed by the ignorant; the cruelest man living could not sit at his feast, unless he sat blindfold. Raise the veil boldly; face the light; and if, as yet, the light of the eye can only be through tears, and the light of the body[72] through sackcloth, go thou forth weeping, bearing precious seed, until the time come, and the kingdom, when Christ's gift of bread, and bequest of peace, shall be "Unto this last as unto thee";[73] and when, for earth's severed multitudes of the wicked and the weary, there shall be holier reconciliation than that of the narrow home, and calm economy, where the Wicked cease—not from trouble, but from troubling—and the Weary are at rest.[74]

---

71. "How great a refreshment there is in asphodel," Hesiod *Works and Days* 40–41. The two lines from which this phrase is taken may be translated as follows: "Fools, they neither know by how much more the half is than the whole nor how great a refreshment there is in mallow and asphodel." Mallow and asphodel are herbs which grow wild in Greece and were the staple diet of the poor in ancient times.

72. Matt. 6:22.

73. Matt. 20:13.

74. Job 3:17.

RENEWALS 691-4574
DATE DUE

SEP 3 0